CAIRO TRAVEL GUIDE 2023 AND BEYOND

Unraveling the Mysteries of Egypt's Timeless Capital

By: Horus Bast

Contents

INTRODUCTION

Welcome to Cairo, a city that stands as a living testament to the wonders of Egypt's timeless past and the vibrancy of its present. Nestled along the banks of the iconic Nile River, Cairo boasts an enchanting fusion of ancient marvels and modern delights. As you embark on a journey through this captivating capital, you'll find yourself unraveling the mysteries of a civilization that has spanned millennia.

With its awe-inspiring Pyramids of Giza, majestic Sphinx, and the treasures of the Egyptian Museum, Cairo invites you to step back in time and witness the grandeur of pharaohs and the ingenuity of ancient architects. Yet, beyond the ancient wonders, the city's beating heart lies in its bustling streets, where the vibrant culture, warm hospitality, and aromatic flavors captivate every visitor.

This travel guide is your key to navigating Cairo's treasures in 2023 and beyond. From the historic mosques and churches of Islamic and Coptic Cairo to the bustling markets of Khan El Khalili, and from serene boat rides along the Nile to the modern art scene and cultural events, Cairo beckons you with an array of experiences to cherish.

So, come with us as we embark on an adventure to unravel the mysteries and embrace the charm of Egypt's captivating capital, where the ancient past meets the dynamic present.

HISTORY OF CAIRO

Cairo's history is long and fascinating, dating back to ancient times. It is one of the oldest cities in the world and has witnessed the rise and fall of numerous civilizations. Here's a brief overview of the history of Cairo:

Ancient Cairo

Ancient Cairo, also known as Old Cairo or Coptic Cairo, is a historic neighborhood located in the southern part of modern-day Cairo. It is a treasure trove of ancient landmarks, religious sites, and cultural heritage that reflects the city's rich history. Here's an overview of Ancient Cairo:

Historical Significance:

Ancient Cairo is one of the oldest parts of the city, with a history that spans over two millennia. It was originally known as "Babylon in Egypt" during Roman and Byzantine times and served as an administrative and military center.

Religious Diversity:

One of the defining features of Ancient Cairo is its religious diversity, housing numerous churches, mosques, and synagogues in close proximity to one another. The neighborhood has been an important center for Christianity, Islam, and Judaism throughout history.

Coptic Christian Heritage:

Ancient Cairo is home to several significant Coptic Christian landmarks, making it an essential pilgrimage site for Coptic Christians from Egypt and around the world. Some of the notable Coptic sites include the Hanging Church (Saint Virgin Mary's Coptic Orthodox Church), the Church of St. Sergius and Bacchus, and the Coptic Museum.

Islamic Heritage:

The neighborhood is dotted with impressive Islamic architecture, including beautiful mosques, madrasas, and mausoleums.

Notable Islamic sites in Ancient Cairo include the Mosque of Amr ibn al-As, the Mosque-Madrassa of Sultan Hassan, and the Mosque of Ibn Tulun.

Jewish History:

While the Jewish community in Cairo has significantly diminished over the centuries, Ancient Cairo still houses a few synagogues, such as the Ben Ezra Synagogue and the Synagogue of Moses Maimonides.

Historic Gates and Walls:

Ancient Cairo was once surrounded by fortified walls and gates. While much of the original fortifications have disappeared, some gates, such as Bab Zuweila and Bab al-Futuh, have survived and stand as reminders of the neighborhood's medieval past.

Cultural Attractions:

In addition to its religious significance, Ancient Cairo offers cultural attractions, including the Khan El-Khalili bazaar, where visitors can shop for traditional handicrafts, textiles, and souvenirs.

Preservation Efforts:

The Egyptian government and various cultural organizations have undertaken efforts to preserve and restore the historical sites in Ancient Cairo, ensuring their cultural significance and heritage are safeguarded for future generations.

Roman and Byzantine Period

The Roman and Byzantine periods in Egypt marked significant chapters in the country's history, shaping its culture, administration, and religious landscape. These periods followed the rule of the pharaohs and preceded the Arab Muslim conquest of Egypt. Here's an overview of the Roman and Byzantine periods in Egypt:

Roman Period (30 BCE - 641 CE):

The Roman period in Egypt began in 30 BCE when Egypt became a province of the Roman Empire after the defeat of Cleopatra VII and Mark Antony by Octavian (later known as Emperor Augustus).

The Roman rule brought significant changes to Egypt's administrative and cultural landscape. The country became an integral part of the vast Roman Empire, with its administrative system, currency, and legal framework reorganized under Roman governance. During the early Roman period, the ancient city of Alexandria remained a thriving center of culture, learning, and trade, attracting scholars and philosophers from various parts of the empire.

Roman emperors, such as Hadrian and Trajan, visited Egypt and left their mark on its architectural landscape, including the construction of temples, theaters, and other public buildings. The Romans also expanded and improved the network of roads and waterways in Egypt, which facilitated trade and communication.

Byzantine Period (641 CE - 642 CE):

The Byzantine period began with the Arab Muslim conquest of Egypt in 641 CE, marking the end of the Roman rule in the region. After the fall of the Western Roman Empire in 476 CE, the Eastern Roman Empire, also known as the Byzantine Empire, continued to exist, with its capital in Constantinople (present-day Istanbul, Turkey).

Egypt became a part of the Byzantine Empire and was ruled by Byzantine governors appointed by the emperor in Constantinople. During the Byzantine period, Egypt's religious landscape witnessed significant changes. The majority of the population gradually converted to Christianity, and Christianity became the dominant religion in the country. The Coptic Church emerged as a significant religious institution in Egypt.

Byzantine rule in Egypt faced challenges, including internal revolts and external threats from Arab Muslim forces. In 642 CE, the Arab Muslim army, led by Amr ibn al-As, successfully captured Alexandria, marking the end of the Byzantine period in Egypt and the beginning of Arab Muslim rule.

Arab Conquest and Foundation of Cairo

The Arab Conquest of Egypt and the foundation of Cairo marked a pivotal moment in Egypt's history, shaping the city's cultural, political, and religious landscape. It was during this time that Cairo, known then as Al-Qahira, was established as the new capital of Egypt. Here's an overview of the Arab Conquest and the foundation of Cairo:

Arab Conquest of Egypt (641 CE):

In the early 7th century CE, the Arab Muslims, led by the general Amr ibn al-As, launched an invasion of Egypt, which was then under Byzantine rule.

The Arab Muslim forces defeated the Byzantine army at the Battle of Heliopolis in 640 CE and subsequently besieged Alexandria, the capital of Egypt at that time.

In 641 CE, Alexandria fell to the Arab Muslim forces, leading to the conquest of Egypt and the end of Byzantine rule in the region.

Foundation of Cairo (969 CE):

After the Arab Conquest, Egypt was part of the vast Islamic Caliphate ruled by the Umayyad and Abbasid Caliphates. In 969 CE, the general Jawhar al-Siqilli, who served under the Fatimid Caliph al-Mu'izz li-Din Allah, founded the new capital of Egypt, Al-Qahira, on the site of the earlier Roman fortress of Babylon in Egypt. Al-Qahira means "The Victorious" in

Arabic, reflecting the Fatimid Caliphate's triumph and the victorious nature of the new capital.

The founding of Al-Qahira was strategic, as it was located between the older cities of Fustat and Al-Askar. These cities served as centers of administration and military power in Egypt during earlier periods. The new city, Al-Qahira, was designed as a grand capital, featuring wide streets, impressive mosques, palaces, and other architectural wonders that reflected the splendor of the Fatimid Caliphate.

The Fatimid Caliphate:

The Fatimid Caliphate, under which Cairo was founded, was a Shia Muslim dynasty that originated from North Africa and claimed descent from the Prophet Muhammad's daughter Fatimah and her husband Ali ibn Abi Talib. The Fatimids were known for their tolerance of different religious groups, including Muslims, Christians, and Jews, and Cairo became a melting pot of diverse cultures and religions.

Fatimid Era

The Fatimid Era was a crucial period in Egyptian history, spanning from 909 CE to 1171 CE. The Fatimid Caliphate was established by the Ismaili Shia Muslims, who traced their lineage to Fatimah, the daughter of the Prophet Muhammad, and her husband Ali ibn Abi Talib. During this time, Egypt was the center of the Fatimid Caliphate's power, and Cairo became its grand capital. Here's an overview of the Fatimid Era:

Establishment of the Fatimid Caliphate (909 CE):

The Fatimid Caliphate was founded in 909 CE by Abdullah al-Mahdi Billah, a descendant of Ali and Fatimah, who proclaimed himself the rightful caliph in North Africa. The Fatimids aimed to challenge the rule of the Abbasid Caliphate in Baghdad and to establish their own Shia Muslim dynasty.

Conquest of Egypt (969 CE):

In 969 CE, the Fatimid general Jawhar al-Siqilli led an army to conquer Egypt, which was then under the rule of the Ikhshidid Dynasty. The Fatimid forces successfully captured Egypt, and Jawhar al-Siqilli founded the new capital, Al-Qahira (Cairo), in 969 CE, marking the beginning of the Fatimid Era in Egypt.

Cultural and Intellectual Flourishing:

The Fatimid Caliphate fostered a period of cultural, intellectual, and architectural flourishing in Egypt. Cairo, as the capital, became a center of learning, attracting scholars, scientists, and intellectuals from different parts of the Islamic world.

Tolerance and Diverse Culture:

The Fatimids were known for their religious tolerance and inclusive policies towards various religious groups, including Muslims, Christians, and Jews. Cairo became a melting pot of cultures and religions, where different communities coexisted and contributed to the city's diverse heritage.

Decline and Ayyubid Conquest:

The Fatimid Caliphate faced internal struggles and political divisions, leading to its decline in the late 11th and early 12th centuries. In 1171 CE, the Ayyubid Dynasty, led by Salah al-Din (Saladin), conquered Egypt and put an end to the Fatimid Caliphate, establishing the Ayyubid rule.

Ayyubid and Mamluk Period

The Ayyubid and Mamluk periods were significant chapters in Egypt's history, characterized by the rule of two powerful dynasties that left a lasting impact on the country's culture, architecture, and political landscape. Here's an overview of the Ayyubid and Mamluk periods in Egypt:

Ayyubid Period (1171 CE - 1250 CE):

The Ayyubid Dynasty was founded by Salah al-Din (Saladin) after he conquered Egypt in 1171 CE. Salah al-Din was a military leader of Kurdish origin and a prominent figure in the Muslim world. Under Ayyubid rule, Egypt and Syria formed a powerful and prosperous empire, with Cairo as its political and cultural center. Salah al-Din's reign is notable for his efforts to unite the Muslim world against the Crusaders and his recapture of Jerusalem in 1187 CE.

Mamluk Period (1250 CE - 1517 CE):

The Mamluk Sultanate was established in 1250 CE after a group of Mamluks (slave soldiers) seized power from the last Ayyubid ruler. The Mamluks were originally slave-soldiers who rose to prominence and eventually became rulers in Egypt and Syria. The Mamluk Sultanate was characterized by strong military leadership and internal political stability, allowing the empire to flourish economically and culturally.

Cairo as a Center of Power:

Both the Ayyubids and Mamluks contributed to the development of Cairo as a grand and prosperous city. They constructed impressive architectural wonders, including mosques, madrasas, palaces, and public buildings that still stand as iconic landmarks in Cairo today. Cairo's religious diversity continued during the Ayyubid and Mamluk periods, with mosques, churches, and synagogues coexisting in harmony.

Economic Prosperity and Trade:

During the Ayyubid and Mamluk periods, Egypt served as a crucial economic hub, benefiting from its strategic location at the crossroads of trade routes between Europe, Africa, and Asia. The flourishing trade brought prosperity to the region, making Cairo a wealthy and cosmopolitan city.

End of the Mamluk Rule:

The Mamluk Sultanate came to an end in 1517 CE when the Ottoman Empire, under Sultan Selim I, defeated the Mamluks in the Battle of Ridaniya. Egypt became a part of the Ottoman Empire, which ruled the country until the early 19th century.

Ottoman Rule

Ottoman Rule in Egypt refers to the period when Egypt was under the control and governance of the Ottoman Empire. It lasted from 1517 CE to 1805 CE and had a significant impact on the country's political, social, and cultural development. Here's an overview of the Ottoman Rule in Egypt:

Conquest of Egypt (1517 CE):

In 1517 CE, the Ottoman Empire, under Sultan Selim I, defeated the Mamluk Sultanate in the Battle of Ridaniya, which led to the conquest of Egypt.

Sultan Selim I officially incorporated Egypt into the Ottoman Empire, and the country became one of its provinces.

Cairo as a Provincial Capital:

Cairo served as the provincial capital during the Ottoman Rule, and the Ottoman governors, known as Beys or Pashas, ruled from the Citadel of Cairo. The city remained an essential administrative, cultural, and religious center within the empire.

Ottoman Influence on Architecture:

The Ottomans left their architectural mark on Cairo, constructing and renovating mosques, public buildings, and fortifications. Some of the notable Ottoman-era landmarks in Cairo include the Mosque of Sultan Suleiman the Magnificent and the historic walls of the city.

Economic and Trade Significance:

During the Ottoman Rule, Egypt remained a crucial economic center, particularly due to its position as a trade hub between Europe, Africa, and Asia. Cairo's economy thrived, attracting merchants and traders from different parts of the world.

Political and Administrative System:

Egypt was ruled by Ottoman governors appointed by the Sultan in Constantinople (Istanbul, Turkey). The Ottoman political system was based on a centralized authority with the Sultan as the ultimate ruler.

Religious and Social Life:

The Ottomans maintained the religious diversity of Cairo, allowing existing religious institutions, such as mosques, churches, and synagogues, to continue operating. Cairo's social life continued to be diverse and cosmopolitan, with various ethnic and religious communities coexisting.

Decline of the Ottoman Empire:

In the 18th and 19th centuries, the Ottoman Empire faced a period of decline known as the Ottoman Decline. The decline of the empire's central authority also affected its control over Egypt, leading to a period of local autonomy.

Mohamed Ali's Rule (1805 - 1848):

In 1805, Mohamed Ali, an ambitious Ottoman governor of Egypt, established his rule, breaking away from direct Ottoman control. Although nominally still under Ottoman suzerainty, Egypt operated as a semi-autonomous state.

2023 and Beyond

Modern Cairo is a bustling metropolis and the capital of Egypt. With a population of over 20 million people, it is one of the largest cities in Africa and the Middle East. Modern Cairo is a vibrant and dynamic city that blends its ancient heritage with the influences of its diverse history. Here's an overview of modern Cairo:

Urbanization and Expansion:

In the 19th and 20th centuries, Cairo experienced significant urbanization and expansion. The city grew rapidly, with new neighborhoods, residential areas, and commercial districts being developed.

Diverse Architecture:

Modern Cairo boasts a diverse architectural landscape, featuring a mix of historic landmarks, colonial-era buildings, and modern skyscrapers.

The city's skyline is adorned with minarets, church domes, and modern towers, creating a unique visual appeal.

Cultural and Educational Hub:

Cairo continues to be a cultural and educational hub in the region. It is home to several universities, museums, art galleries, and theaters that contribute to Egypt's vibrant cultural scene.

Economic Center:

Cairo serves as the economic center of Egypt, housing the country's major businesses, financial institutions, and government offices.

The city's economy is diverse, with industries ranging from textiles and manufacturing to tourism and information technology.

Traffic and Transportation:

Cairo faces traffic congestion due to its high population density and the sheer number of vehicles on the road.

The city has an extensive public transportation system, including buses, an underground metro, and microbuses.

Global and Regional Influence:

Cairo plays a pivotal role in regional and international affairs. It hosts major summits, conferences, and diplomatic meetings, making it a significant diplomatic hub in the Arab world.

Cultural Heritage:

Despite its modernization, Cairo has preserved its rich cultural heritage. Ancient landmarks, such as the Giza Pyramids, the Egyptian Museum, and the historic mosques and churches, continue to attract visitors from around the world.

Contemporary Lifestyle:

Modern Cairo has a vibrant nightlife, with numerous restaurants, cafes, and entertainment venues catering to a diverse range of tastes.

The city offers a blend of traditional and contemporary elements, creating a unique lifestyle experience for residents and visitors alike.

Challenges and Opportunities:

Like any major city, Cairo faces challenges, including overpopulation, pollution, and urban development issues.

However, the city also presents numerous opportunities for growth, innovation, and cultural exchange.

IMPORTANT INFORMATION

Visa Requirements

The visa requirements for traveling to Egypt vary depending on your nationality and the purpose of your visit. Here are some general guidelines:

Visa on Arrival

Citizens of many countries can obtain a visa on arrival at Cairo International Airport and other major entry points in Egypt. This visa is typically valid for a stay of up to 30 days. However, it's essential to check if your country is eligible for visa on arrival before traveling.

E-Visa

F-Some countries have the option to apply for an e-visa before traveling to Egypt. The e-visa allows you to complete the visa application online and obtain an electronic visa that you can print and present upon arrival.

Visa in Advance

In some cases, travelers from certain countries are required to obtain a visa from an Egyptian embassy or consulate in their home country before departure. This is especially true for those planning to stay for an extended period or for specific purposes like work or study.

Tourist Visa Extension

If you wish to extend your stay beyond the initial visa period, you can apply for an extension at the Egyptian Passport and Immigration Office in Cairo or other cities.

Climate and Best Time to Visit

Cairo experiences a desert climate with hot, dry summers and mild winters. The best time to visit Cairo is during the cooler months when the weather is more pleasant for outdoor activities and sightseeing. Here's a breakdown of Cairo's climate and the recommended time to visit:

Spring (March to May)

Spring is one of the best times to visit Cairo. The weather is mild and comfortable, with temperatures ranging from 18°C to 28°C (64°F to 82°F). The city comes alive with blooming flowers, and it's an excellent time for exploring the historical sites and enjoying outdoor activities.

Autumn (September to November)

Another ideal time to visit Cairo is during the autumn months. Temperatures start to cool down after the hot summer, ranging from 20°C to 30°C (68°F to 86°F). It's a great time for sightseeing and experiencing the city's vibrant cultural scene.

Summer (June to August)

Summer in Cairo can be scorching, with temperatures soaring above 35°C (95°F) and often reaching 40°C (104°F) or higher. It can be uncomfortably hot for outdoor activities, and sightseeing might be challenging during the peak of the day. If you visit in summer, be prepared for intense heat and consider indoor attractions or evening outings.

Winter (December to February)

Cairo's winters are mild compared to many other parts of the world, but it can still get chilly at night. Daytime temperatures range from 14°C to 22°C (57°F to 72°F). While it's a good time to explore the city without the scorching heat, be sure to pack some layers for the cooler evenings.

Currency

The local currency of Egypt is the Egyptian Pound, abbreviated as EGP or LE (short for Livre Égyptienne). The currency is issued and regulated by the Central Bank of Egypt. Here are some key points to know about the Egyptian Pound:

Denominations

The Egyptian Pound is available in both coins and banknotes. Coins are available in denominations of 1, 5, 10, 20, 25, and 50 Piasters, as well as 1 Pound. Banknotes are issued in denominations of 5, 10, 20, 50, 100, 200, and 500 Pounds.

Value

The exchange rate of the Egyptian Pound varies against other currencies, such as the US Dollar, Euro, or British Pound. It's advisable to check the current exchange rate before exchanging your money.

Exchanging Currency

You can exchange your foreign currency for Egyptian Pounds at banks, official currency exchange offices, or authorized hotels. Major airports and tourist areas also have currency exchange services, but rates may not be as favorable.

ATMs and Credit Cards

ATMs are widely available in Cairo and other major cities, and most accept international credit and debit cards. However, it's always a good idea to inform your bank about your travel plans to avoid any issues with card usage.

Cash vs. Cards

While credit and debit cards are generally accepted at larger establishments and hotels, it's a good idea to carry some cash, especially for smaller purchases and at local markets where cash is preferred.

Currency Restrictions

There are no restrictions on bringing foreign currency into Egypt. However, if you plan to take more than 5,000 Egyptian Pounds out of the country, you must declare it upon departure.

Language

The official language of Egypt is Arabic. Arabic is spoken by the majority of the population and is used in all official and government communications. Here are some key points about the language in Egypt:

Egyptian Colloquial Arabic

While Modern Standard Arabic (MSA) is the formal version of Arabic used in media, literature, and education, the everyday language spoken by Egyptians is Egyptian Colloquial Arabic (also known as Masri). It has its unique pronunciation, vocabulary, and grammar compared to MSA.

English Proficiency

In urban areas and popular tourist destinations, you will find many Egyptians who can speak English, especially those working in the tourism industry, hotels, restaurants, and shops. English is taught in schools and is the second most commonly used language for communication with international visitors.

Communication Tips

While English can be widely understood, learning a few basic Arabic phrases can be beneficial and appreciated by the locals. Simple greetings like "hello" (Marhaba), "thank you" (Shukran), and "please" (Min Fadlak for males and Min Fadlik for females) can go a long way in showing respect and building rapport.

Arabic Script

Arabic is written in the Arabic script, which reads from right to left. It's a beautiful and elegant script, but if you're not familiar with it, reading signs or written text can be challenging for non-Arabic speakers.

Multilingual Signage

In major tourist areas, you will often find signs, menus, and information in both Arabic and English, making it easier for travelers to navigate.

Dialect Variations

Keep in mind that Arabic dialects can vary from one region to another within Egypt and other Arab countries. While Egyptian Colloquial Arabic is widely understood throughout Egypt, some regional variations may exist.

Language of Religion

Arabic is also the language of Islam, and many religious texts and prayers are in Arabic. However, most mosques in tourist areas have translations or guidebooks available for visitors.

Health and Safety

Health and safety are crucial aspects to consider while traveling to Cairo or any destination. Here are some important tips to ensure a safe and enjoyable trip:

Travel Insurance

Before your trip, make sure you have comprehensive travel insurance that covers medical emergencies, trip cancellations, and other unforeseen circumstances.

Drinking Water

Drink bottled water and avoid tap water, especially in Cairo. Staying hydrated is essential, especially during the hot months.

Food Safety

Be cautious with food hygiene, especially when eating street food. Opt for freshly cooked and hot meals from reputable vendors.

Sun Protection

Cairo can get very hot, especially in the summer. Wear sunscreen, a hat, and sunglasses to protect yourself from the sun.

Traffic Safety

Cairo's streets can be busy and chaotic, with heavy traffic. Exercise caution when crossing roads and consider using designated pedestrian crossings.

COVID-19 Precautions

Stay updated on the latest COVID-19 travel guidelines and requirements for Egypt. Follow local health protocols, wear masks when required, and maintain social distancing.

Avoiding Scams

Be aware of common scams targeting tourists, such as overcharging for goods or services. Always agree on prices before taking a taxi or purchasing items.

Petty Theft

Keep your belongings secure and be cautious in crowded areas, as pickpocketing can occur.

Political Demonstrations

While political demonstrations in Cairo have been infrequent, it's essential to stay informed about the local situation and avoid large gatherings if they occur.

Pharmacies

Locate pharmacies in the area you are staying in case you need over-the-counter medications or medical assistance.

Personal Health

If you have any pre-existing medical conditions, bring enough medication for your trip and carry a medical information card with your relevant health information.

Vaccinations

Before traveling to Cairo, it is essential to check with your healthcare provider or a travel medicine specialist to determine which vaccinations are recommended or required for your trip. The recommended vaccinations may vary based on factors such as your health status, previous immunizations, the duration of your stay, and the specific activities you plan to undertake in Egypt. Here are some vaccinations commonly recommended for travelers to Egypt:

Routine Vaccinations

Ensure that you are up-to-date on routine vaccinations, including measles, mumps, rubella, diphtheria, tetanus, pertussis, polio, and varicella (chickenpox).

Hepatitis A

This vaccination is recommended for all travelers to Egypt, as the virus can be contracted through contaminated food and water.

Hepatitis B

Hepatitis B vaccination is recommended for travelers who may have intimate contact with locals, require medical treatment, or engage in activities that may expose them to blood or bodily fluids.

Typhoid

The typhoid vaccination is advised for travelers who plan to consume food or drink from potentially contaminated sources.

Rabies

If you plan to have significant contact with animals or participate in outdoor activities that might put you at risk for animal bites, a rabies vaccination may be recommended.

Yellow Fever

Yellow fever vaccination is required for travelers coming from or transiting through yellow fever-endemic countries. Egypt itself is not a yellow fever-endemic country.

Transportation

Getting around Cairo can be an adventure in itself due to the city's bustling streets and traffic congestion. However, there are several transportation options available to help you navigate the city and explore its many attractions:

Metro

Cairo has a modern and efficient metro system, which is one of the fastest and most affordable ways to get around the city.

The metro connects various neighborhoods and key tourist sites, including the Egyptian Museum and Coptic Cairo. It's a convenient option during rush hours when traffic can be heavy.

Taxis

Taxis are readily available throughout Cairo, and they can be hailed from the street or found at designated taxi stands. Make sure the taxi driver uses the meter, or negotiate the fare before starting your journey. Uber and other ride-sharing services are also popular in Cairo and provide a reliable alternative to regular taxis.

Microbuses

Microbuses are small vans or minivans that operate on fixed routes throughout the city. They are a budget-friendly option, but they can get crowded and are not always the most comfortable mode of transportation.

Buses

Cairo has an extensive bus network that covers various parts of the city. However, buses can be crowded, and the schedules may not always be reliable, especially during peak hours.

Trams

Some parts of Cairo, such as Heliopolis, have a tram system that provides another option for public transportation.

Nile River Boats (Feluccas)

Enjoy a traditional boat ride on the Nile River with a felucca cruise. While feluccas are not used for daily transportation, they offer a unique and relaxing way to experience the river and enjoy views of Cairo's landmarks.

Rental Cars

While driving in Cairo can be challenging due to traffic and local driving habits, you can rent a car if you feel comfortable navigating the city on your own. Make sure to have a GPS or a reliable map to help you find your way around.

Walking and Cycling

Depending on your location, walking or cycling can be a viable option for getting around certain areas of Cairo, especially in downtown and more pedestrian-friendly neighborhoods.

Accommodation

Cairo offers a wide range of accommodation options to suit different budgets and preferences. Whether you're looking for luxury hotels with stunning views of the Nile, charming boutique guesthouses in historic neighborhoods, or budget-friendly hostels for backpackers, Cairo has something to offer. Here are some types of accommodation you can consider:

Luxury Hotels

Cairo boasts several world-class luxury hotels that cater to discerning travelers. These hotels often feature opulent interiors, excellent dining options, spa facilities, and stunning views of the city or the Nile River.

Mid-Range Hotels

There are numerous mid-range hotels in Cairo that provide comfortable accommodations and amenities at more affordable prices. These hotels are a popular choice for many travelers seeking a balance between comfort and budget.

Budget Hotels and Guesthouses

If you're looking for more affordable options, you'll find a variety of budget hotels and guesthouses in Cairo. These accommodations offer basic amenities, clean rooms, and a friendly atmosphere.

Hostels

Cairo has several hostels that cater to backpackers and budget-conscious travelers. Hostels are an excellent choice for meeting fellow travelers and can provide a fun and social experience.

Airbnb and Vacation Rentals

Many visitors to Cairo opt for Airbnb or vacation rentals, especially if they are looking for a more home-like experience. Renting an apartment or a private room in someone's home can offer a unique and immersive experience in the local culture.

Nile River Cruises

For a different kind of accommodation, consider a Nile River cruise. These cruises offer the chance to explore the sights along the Nile while enjoying the comfort of a floating hotel.

Boutique Hotels

Cairo has some charming boutique hotels with character and unique design elements. These smaller properties often offer personalized service and a more intimate ambiance.

Dress Code

Cairo, being a Muslim-majority city, has a conservative dress code, especially when visiting religious sites and more traditional neighborhoods. While the dress code in Cairo is generally more relaxed compared to some other Middle Eastern cities, it's essential to respect local customs and cultural norms. Here are some guidelines for appropriate dress in Cairo:

Modest Clothing

When visiting mosques, churches, or other religious sites, both men and women should dress modestly. This means avoiding clothing that is too revealing, such as shorts, tank tops, and sleeveless shirts.

Covered Shoulders and Knees

It's advisable for both men and women to cover their shoulders and knees when visiting religious sites and conservative areas.

Scarves for Women

Women may want to carry a lightweight scarf to cover their heads when entering mosques as a sign of respect. Some mosques provide scarves at the entrance for female visitors.

Casual Clothing

For everyday activities and sightseeing, casual clothing like loose-fitting trousers or skirts, t-shirts, and blouses is generally acceptable. However, avoid overly tight or revealing clothing, especially in more traditional areas.

Swimwear

While it's fine to wear swimwear at hotel pools or private resorts, it's not appropriate to wear revealing swimwear in public areas or outside designated beach areas.

Dressing for the Weather

Take the weather into account when dressing. Cairo can get very hot, especially in the summer, so lightweight, breathable fabrics are recommended.

Footwear

Comfortable walking shoes are a must, as you'll likely do a lot of exploring on foot. Sandals are also a good option, especially in warmer months.

Respect Local Customs

Remember that Cairo is a conservative city, and dressing appropriately shows respect for the local culture and religious beliefs.

Local Customs

When visiting Cairo, it's essential to be mindful of the local customs and traditions to show respect for the local culture and ensure a positive and enjoyable experience. Here are some important local customs to keep in mind:

Greetings

Greetings are an essential part of Egyptian culture. When meeting someone, it's customary to exchange greetings with a handshake, especially between members of the same sex. Men may greet each other with a handshake and a kiss on each cheek. However, physical contact between men and women who are not related is generally avoided.

Hospitality

Egyptians are known for their warm hospitality and generosity towards guests. If invited to someone's home, it's polite to bring a small gift, such as sweets, fruits, or flowers, as a token of appreciation.

Respect for Religion

Egypt is a predominantly Muslim country, and Islam plays a significant role in the lives of the people. When visiting mosques or other religious sites, dress modestly and remove your shoes before entering. Women may be required to cover their heads with a scarf. Always be respectful during prayer times and avoid taking photos without permission.

Public Displays of Affection

Public displays of affection, such as hugging or kissing, are not common in Egyptian culture. It's best to avoid such behavior in public to adhere to local customs.

Feet and Shoes

The feet are considered the lowest part of the body, both physically and symbolically. Avoid pointing the soles of your feet at others, as it is considered impolite. When entering someone's home or a mosque, always remove your shoes.

Use of the Right Hand

In Middle Eastern cultures, the left hand is traditionally associated with personal hygiene and is considered unclean. Therefore, when eating, offering gifts, or interacting with others, use your right hand.

Photography

Always ask for permission before taking photos of people, especially women, and respect their decision if they decline. In some areas, photography may be restricted, particularly near military installations or sensitive sites.

Bargaining

Bargaining is a common practice in markets and souks. Polite haggling is part of the shopping experience, but remember to be respectful and avoid overly aggressive bargaining.

Time Flexibility

Egyptians often have a more relaxed approach to time. It's not uncommon for appointments or meetings to start later than scheduled. Be patient and flexible with time-related matters.

Arabic Phrases

While English is widely spoken in tourist areas, learning a few basic Arabic phrases can be appreciated by the locals and help you connect better with the culture.

Photography

Photography in Cairo can be a rewarding experience, allowing you to capture the city's rich history, stunning landmarks, and vibrant street life. However, it's essential to be mindful of local customs and regulations when taking photos. Here are some tips for photography in Cairo:

Ask for Permission

Always ask for permission before taking photos of people, especially when photographing individuals up close or in more intimate settings. Respect their privacy and cultural sensitivities. Some locals may decline to be photographed, and it's essential to honor their wishes.

Respect Religious Sites

When visiting mosques, churches, or other religious sites, be mindful of the rules regarding photography. Some places may restrict photography inside prayer halls or during specific religious ceremonies. Always follow any signs or instructions provided by the site's management.

Avoid Sensitive Locations

Refrain from taking photos near military installations, government buildings, or other sensitive areas. Photography may be restricted in such places, and attempting to take pictures could lead to unwanted attention or legal issues.

Be Discreet in Crowded Places

In busy and crowded areas, exercise caution when taking photos to avoid accidentally capturing people who may not wish to be photographed. Be aware of your surroundings and respect the privacy of others.

Street Photography

Cairo's streets offer fantastic opportunities for street photography, capturing the daily life, bustling markets, and colorful scenes. However, always be respectful and discreet when photographing people in public spaces.

Consider Cultural Sensitivities

Respect local customs and dress codes when photographing people or religious sites. Be cautious about photographing women without their permission, especially in conservative areas.

Avoid Offensive Content

Refrain from taking photos that may be considered offensive or disrespectful to the local culture, religion, or traditions.

Engage with Locals

Interact with the locals and build rapport before taking their photos. Engaging in conversation and showing genuine interest in their lives can lead to more natural and authentic photographs.

Share Your Photos Responsibly

If you plan to share your photos on social media or online platforms, be mindful of the content and how it may be perceived by others. Avoid sharing photos that could be seen as disrespectful or intrusive.

Bargaining

Bargaining, also known as haggling, is a common practice in Cairo's markets (souks) and many other parts of Egypt. It's an integral part of the shopping experience and can be an enjoyable way to interact with local vendors while getting the best price for your purchases. Here are some tips for bargaining in Cairo:

Start with a Smile

Approach the bargaining process with a friendly and positive attitude. A warm smile and polite greeting can set a friendly tone for the negotiation.

Know the Local Currency

Familiarize yourself with the local currency (Egyptian Pound) and its approximate value in your home currency. This will help you understand the worth of the items you are interested in purchasing.

Do Your Research

Before heading to the markets, research the approximate price range for the items you plan to buy. Knowing the general market value will give you a starting point for negotiations.

Be Polite and Respectful

Always be respectful to the vendor and maintain a polite demeanor throughout the bargaining process. Being rude or aggressive is not likely to result in a favorable outcome.

Start with a Low Offer

Begin by offering a price significantly lower than the vendor's initial asking price. This is a standard part of the bargaining process, and vendors usually expect some negotiation.

Counteroffers and Incremental Increases

The vendor will likely counter your offer with a higher price. Gradually increase your offer in small increments while continuing to show interest in the item.

Walk Away if Necessary

If you reach a point where you cannot agree on a price and feel that the vendor's asking price is not reasonable, don't be afraid to walk away. This can sometimes prompt the vendor to offer a better deal to keep you as a potential customer.

Be Prepared to Compromise

Bargaining is about finding a middle ground that both you and the vendor are satisfied with. Be open to compromise and be willing to meet somewhere between your initial offer and the vendor's counteroffer.

Be Mindful of Quality

While negotiating for a lower price is common, be mindful of the quality of the item you are purchasing. Ensure that you are still getting a fair deal for the product's value and condition.

Enjoy the Experience

Bargaining can be a fun and engaging part of shopping in Cairo. Embrace the process and enjoy the interaction with the vendors, as it can lead to memorable experiences and interesting conversations.

Tipping

Tipping is a common practice in Egypt and is an important aspect of the local culture. Many workers in the service industry rely on tips as a significant part of their income. Here are some tipping guidelines to follow while in Cairo:

Restaurants, Cafés, and Hotels

It's customary to leave a tip for the service staff. A 10-15% tip of the total bill is generally considered appropriate. Some restaurants may include a service charge on the bill, so check before adding an additional tip.

Tour Guides and Drivers

If you hire a tour guide or driver for a private tour or excursion, it's customary to tip them for their services. The amount of the tip can vary based on the length and quality of the service but is typically around 5-10% of the total cost of the tour.

Taxi Drivers

Tipping taxi drivers is not mandatory, but it's common to round up the fare or leave a small tip as a gesture of appreciation for the ride.

Security

Security is an important aspect to consider when traveling to Cairo or any destination. While Cairo is generally safe for tourists, like any major city, it's essential to take some precautions to ensure your safety and have a smooth trip. Here are some security tips for traveling to Cairo:

Stay Informed

Before your trip, check for any travel advisories or safety updates from your government's foreign affairs department. Stay informed about the local situation and any potential security risks.

Choose Accommodation Wisely

Opt for reputable and well-reviewed hotels or accommodations in safe neighborhoods. Research the area's safety and accessibility to key attractions.

Secure Your Belongings

Keep your valuables and important documents secure at all times. Use hotel safes when available and avoid carrying large amounts of cash or displaying expensive items in public.

Be Cautious in Crowded Areas

Be aware of your surroundings, especially in crowded places like markets and tourist attractions. Petty theft can occur in crowded areas, so keep a close eye on your belongings.

Avoid Demonstrations and Protests

While political demonstrations in Cairo are not as frequent as in the past, it's advisable to avoid participating in or getting too close to any political protests or large gatherings.

Use Licensed Transportation

When using taxis or other forms of transportation, use official and licensed services. Avoid accepting rides from unmarked vehicles or strangers.

Electrical Outlets

In Cairo, Egypt, the standard voltage is 220-240 volts, and the frequency is 50 Hz. The electrical outlets used in Egypt are of the two-round-pin type, similar to the European standard Type C and Type F outlets. Here are some details about the electrical outlets in Cairo:

The most common type of electrical plug used in Cairo and throughout Egypt is the Europlug (Type C) and the Schuko plug (Type F). The Europlug has two round pins, while the Schuko plug has two round pins with two earth clips on the side.

If your home country uses a different type of plug or operates on a different voltage, you will need a travel adapter and possibly a voltage converter to use your electronic devices in Egypt. Most modern electronic devices, such as smartphones, laptops, and camera chargers, are dual-voltage and can handle both 110-120V and 220-240V. However, always check the voltage requirements on your specific devices before plugging them in.

Many hotels in Cairo offer both Type C and Type F outlets, as well as some standard international outlets (Type A/B), to accommodate guests from different regions. However, it's always a good idea to carry a travel adapter with you to be prepared.

Internet and Communication

Internet and communication services in Cairo have significantly improved in recent years, offering visitors and residents good connectivity options. Here are some key points to know about internet and communication in Cairo:

Internet Availability

High-speed internet is widely available in Cairo, especially in hotels, restaurants, cafes, and major tourist areas. Many accommodations offer complimentary Wi-Fi for guests.

Mobile Data

Egypt has well-established mobile networks, and you can easily get a local SIM card with a data plan from major providers like Vodafone, Orange, or Etisalat. This allows you to have internet access on your smartphone throughout the city.

Internet Cafes

Internet cafes are still available in some areas of Cairo, but they are less common nowadays due to the widespread availability of mobile data and Wi-Fi.

Communication Apps

Messaging and communication apps like WhatsApp, Telegram, and Facebook Messenger are widely used in Cairo for staying in touch with friends and family, both locally and internationally.

VoIP Services

Voice over Internet Protocol (VoIP) services like Skype and WhatsApp calls are accessible in Cairo. However, their availability and quality of service may vary, as there have been occasional restrictions on VoIP services in the past.

Postal Services

Cairo has a functioning postal system, and you can send and receive mail from various post offices throughout the city.

Language Barrier

While English is commonly spoken, especially in tourist areas and among the younger population, there might still be some language barriers, especially when communicating with locals who are not familiar with English.

Emergency Numbers

The emergency numbers in Egypt are 122 for police, 123 for ambulance, and 180 for tourist police. It's a good idea to save these numbers in your phone in case of any emergencies.

Public Wi-Fi

Some public places, like airports and shopping malls, may offer free public Wi-Fi, but it's essential to use caution when connecting to open networks to protect your data.

Emergency Numbers

In Egypt, including Cairo, the emergency contact numbers for police, ambulance, and tourist police are as follows:

❖ Police: 122

❖ Ambulance: 123

❖ Tourist Police: 180

Time Zone

Cairo, Egypt, is in the Eastern European Time (EET) time zone. During standard time, Cairo is 2 hours ahead of Coordinated Universal Time (UTC+2). However, please note that Egypt observes daylight saving time, which means that during the summer months, the clocks are set one hour ahead, making Cairo 3 hours ahead of Coordinated Universal Time (UTC+3).

Daylight saving time in Egypt typically starts at the end of April or early May and ends at the end of September or early October. During daylight saving time, Cairo follows the Eastern European Summer Time (EEST) time zone.

It's always a good idea to check the current local time in Cairo before your trip, especially if you are coordinating with people in different time zones or have time-sensitive appointments or activities planned.

Cultural Sensitivity

Cultural sensitivity is of utmost importance when traveling to Cairo or any foreign destination. Being culturally sensitive means respecting and understanding the local customs, traditions, beliefs, and behaviors of the people in the host country. Here are some tips for being culturally sensitive while in Cairo:

Greeting Etiquette

Learn and use common Arabic greetings like "As-salamu alaykum" (peace be upon you) when appropriate. Handshakes are commonly used, but be aware of gender-specific greetings in certain situations.

Religious Sites

When visiting mosques or churches, follow the rules and guidelines set by the religious authorities. Respect prayer times and avoid loud or disruptive behavior.

Photography

Always ask for permission before taking photos of people, especially in more intimate or private settings. Be aware of local sensitivities about photography in certain areas.

Ramadan

If you visit Cairo during Ramadan, the Islamic holy month of fasting, be respectful of those who are observing the fast. Avoid eating, drinking, or smoking in public during daylight hours.

Public Affection

Public displays of affection are not commonly practiced in Egyptian culture. Show restraint in displaying affection in public.

Language

Attempt to learn a few basic Arabic phrases to show respect and appreciation for the local language and culture. However, don't assume that everyone speaks English, so be patient in communicating.

Cultural Differences

Be open-minded and understanding of cultural differences. What might be acceptable or common in your home country may not be the same in Egypt.

Personal Space

Be mindful of personal space, especially with people of the opposite gender. Avoid prolonged eye contact or touching that may make others uncomfortable.

Handling Religious Items

If you are invited into someone's home or a religious establishment, be careful when handling religious items or artifacts, and always seek permission if you wish to take photographs.

Arabic phrases

Learning a few basic Arabic phrases can go a long way in showing respect and appreciation for the local language and culture in Cairo. Here are some essential phrases to help you communicate with locals:

* Hello: مرحباً (Marhaban) - pronounced "mar-ha-ban"

* Thank you: شكرًا (Shukran) - pronounced "shook-ran"

* Yes: نعم (Na'am) - pronounced "nah-am"

* No: لا (La) - pronounced "la"

* Please: من فضلك (Min Fadlak) - pronounced "min fad-lak" (when speaking to a male), or من فضلكِ (Min Fadlik) - pronounced "min fad-leek" (when speaking to a female)

* Excuse me / Sorry: عذرًا (Adharaan) - pronounced "ad-ha-ran"

* How much?: بكم؟ (Bikam?) - pronounced "bee-kam?"

* Where is...?: أين ...؟ (Ayna...?) - pronounced "ay-na...?"

* I don't understand: أنا لا أفهم (Ana la afham) - pronounced "a-na la af-ham"

* Goodbye: وداعًا (Wada'an) - pronounced "wa-da-an"

* My name is...: اسمي ... (Ismi...) - pronounced "is-mee..."

* Can you help me?: هل يمكنك مساعدتي؟ (Hal yumkinuka musa'adati?) - pronounced "hal yoom-kee-noo-ka moo-sa-ad-a-tee?"

* I'm sorry, I don't speak Arabic: آسف، لا أتكلم العربية (Aasif, laa atakallam al-'arabiya) - pronounced "a-sif, la a-ta-kal-lam al-ar-a-bi-ya"

❖ Cheers! (for toasting): صحتك فى (Fi sahetak) - pronounced "fee sa-ha-tak"

❖ Yes, please / No, thank you: نعم من فضلك / لا، شكرًا (Na'am, min fadlak / La, shukran) - pronounced "na'am, min fad-lak / la, shook-ran"

CAIRO'S CULTURE

airo's culture is a rich tapestry that reflects the city's long and diverse history. As the capital and largest city of Egypt, Cairo has been a center of cultural, political, and economic activity for millennia. Its cultural heritage is deeply intertwined with the ancient Egyptian civilization, Islamic traditions, Coptic Christianity, and a blend of various influences from the Mediterranean, Africa, and the Middle East. Here are some key aspects of Cairo's culture:

Egyptian Music and Dance

Egyptian music and dance have a rich and diverse history, deeply rooted in the country's ancient culture and influenced by various civilizations over the centuries. Egyptian music and dance are characterized by their vibrant rhythms, expressive movements, and the fusion of different styles and traditions. Here's an overview of Egyptian music and dance:

Egyptian Music

Traditional Egyptian music is known for its use of various instruments, including the oud (a stringed instrument), qanun (a plucked zither), ney (a flute), violin, and tabla (drums). The maqamat system is an essential aspect of Egyptian music, involving a set of melodic modes that form the basis for improvisation and performance. Different genres of Egyptian music exist, such as classical (tarab), folk, religious (Sufi), and contemporary pop music. Classical music, with its soulful and emotional melodies, has been influential in shaping Egyptian musical traditions.

Traditional Egyptian Dance

Raqs Sharqi, commonly known as belly dance, is one of the most famous traditional Egyptian dance forms. It is characterized by fluid and sinuous movements of the hips, abdomen, and arms, often performed by female dancers. Tahtib is a traditional male dance originating from Upper Egypt, involving the use of a long stick as a prop. Tahtib displays martial-like movements and is often accompanied by traditional music. Tanoura is a Sufi-inspired folk dance where male performers whirl and spin in colorful skirts, symbolizing spiritual enlightenment and a connection with the divine.

Saidi Dance

Saidi dance is a traditional folk dance from Upper Egypt, particularly from the Said region (Southern Egypt). It is often performed by both men and women during festive occasions. The dance involves strong and vigorous movements, including cane dancing, where the performer skillfully twirls and tosses a cane while dancing.

Modern and Pop Music

Egypt has a thriving contemporary music scene, encompassing various genres like pop, rock, hip-hop, and rap. Egyptian pop music often blends traditional elements with modern beats and styles. Many Egyptian artists have gained international recognition, contributing to the country's vibrant music industry.

Cairo's Traffic

Cairo's traffic is notorious for its congestion and chaotic nature. As one of the largest and most populous cities in the world, Cairo faces significant traffic challenges due to its rapid urbanization, population growth, and limited road infrastructure. Here are some key aspects of Cairo's traffic:

Congestion

Cairo's streets and highways are often congested with heavy traffic, particularly during rush hours, which can extend for several hours in the morning and evening. The high volume of vehicles on the roads contributes to frequent gridlocks and slow-moving traffic.

Lack of Infrastructure

Cairo's road infrastructure struggles to keep up with the increasing number of vehicles on the streets. Many roads are narrow and poorly maintained, and there is a lack of modern transportation systems, such as an efficient public transit network.

Informal Driving Culture

Cairo's traffic is characterized by an informal driving culture, with many drivers disregarding traffic rules and regulations. Lane discipline, speed limits, and traffic signals are often ignored, leading to disorderly traffic flow.

Traffic Accidents

The chaotic traffic conditions in Cairo contribute to a higher risk of traffic accidents. Reckless driving, lack of enforcement of traffic laws, and poorly maintained vehicles are some factors that increase the likelihood of accidents.

Public Transportation Challenges

While Cairo has a public transportation system, including buses and a metro system, it still faces challenges in meeting the demand of the city's massive population. Many commuters rely on private cars, further contributing to traffic congestion.

Informal Transportation

In addition to formal public transportation, informal modes of transportation, such as microbuses and tuk-tuks, are prevalent in Cairo. While they offer flexibility and accessibility, they can also add to traffic congestion and pose safety risks.

Urban Planning Issues

Rapid urbanization and informal settlements in Cairo have led to haphazard city planning and inadequate road design, exacerbating traffic problems.

Efforts to Improve Traffic

The Egyptian government has implemented various initiatives to alleviate traffic congestion, including expanding and upgrading road infrastructure, introducing traffic management systems, and promoting public transportation. However, addressing the issue requires long-term and comprehensive planning.

Cairo's Street Food Delights

Cairo's street food scene is a delight for food lovers, offering a diverse array of delicious and flavorful dishes that showcase the rich culinary heritage of Egypt. The bustling streets of Cairo are filled with food vendors and stalls, each offering their unique specialties. Here are some must-try street food delights in Cairo:

Falafel

Falafel is a popular Middle Eastern dish made from ground chickpeas or fava beans mixed with herbs and spices, formed into balls, and deep-fried until crispy. It is often served in a pita bread with tahini sauce, salad, and pickles.

Koshari

Koshari is a classic Egyptian comfort food and a must-try street food. It is a hearty dish made with layers of rice, lentils, macaroni, and chickpeas, topped with crispy fried onions and a spicy tomato sauce.

Shawarma

Shawarma is a delicious street food made from thinly sliced marinated meat (usually beef, chicken, or lamb) cooked on a vertical rotisserie. The meat is usually served in a flatbread wrap with garlic sauce, tahini, and vegetables.

Ful Medames

Ful medames is a traditional Egyptian dish made from cooked fava beans seasoned with garlic, lemon juice, and olive oil. It is often served as a hearty breakfast dish with bread and vegetables.

Ta'ameya

Ta'ameya is the Egyptian version of falafel, made with ground fava beans, herbs, and spices. It has a distinct flavor and is usually served in a pita bread with salad and tahini sauce.

Grilled Corn

Grilled corn on the cob is a popular street snack in Cairo. The corn is usually grilled over charcoal and seasoned with salt, lemon, and spices.

Sambousek

Sambousek is a delicious pastry filled with meat, cheese, or vegetables. It is often deep-fried and served as a savory snack.

Basbousa

Basbousa is a sweet semolina cake soaked in simple syrup and flavored with coconut and sometimes nuts. It is a popular dessert often found in Cairo's street food markets.

Zalabya

Zalabya is a type of deep-fried sweet dough pastry shaped into small balls or spirals and soaked in syrup. It is a popular sweet treat sold by street vendors.

Baladi Bread

Baladi bread, also known as Egyptian flatbread, is a staple in Cairo's street food scene. It is served with almost every meal and used to wrap various dishes, such as falafel, shawarma, and ta'ameya.

Cairo's Fashion and Textiles

Cairo's fashion and textiles industry is a vibrant and diverse sector that reflects the city's rich cultural heritage and influences from various historical periods. From traditional attire to contemporary fashion, Cairo offers a wide range of styles and textiles that cater to both local and international markets. Here are some key aspects of Cairo's fashion and textiles:

Traditional Egyptian Clothing

Traditional Egyptian clothing includes garments like the galabeya, a loose-fitting, ankle-length tunic often worn by both men and women. The galabeya is commonly made of cotton and is perfect for the hot climate of Cairo.

Islamic Clothing

As a predominantly Muslim country, Islamic clothing is prevalent in Cairo. Women often wear the hijab (headscarf) and modest dresses, while men may wear the thobe (long tunic) and kufi (a rounded cap).

Textile Industry

Cairo has a thriving textile industry that produces a variety of fabrics, including cotton, linen, silk, and wool. Egyptian cotton is particularly renowned for its softness and high quality.

Souks and Markets

Cairo's souks and markets are treasure troves for textiles and fabrics. Khan El Khalili, one of the oldest markets in the city, is a popular destination for purchasing fabrics, scarves, and other textiles.

Embroidery and Handicrafts

Traditional Egyptian embroidery and handicrafts play a significant role in the local fashion scene. Intricate designs and patterns adorn garments and accessories, adding a unique touch to the textiles.

Contemporary Fashion

Cairo has a growing contemporary fashion scene, with local designers blending traditional elements with modern aesthetics. Fashion boutiques, design studios, and fashion events contribute to the city's evolving fashion landscape.

Coptic Textiles

Cairo's Coptic Christian community has a rich history of textile production, with some of the earliest known Christian textiles originating from Egypt. Coptic textiles often feature intricate woven patterns and designs.

Influence of Pharaonic Culture

The ancient Egyptian civilization continues to inspire contemporary fashion and textile designs in Cairo. Motifs, symbols, and patterns from ancient Egypt find their way into modern clothing and accessories.

Global Presence

Cairo's fashion and textiles industry has a global reach, with Egyptian textiles exported to various parts of the world. Cairo also hosts international fashion events and exhibitions that attract designers and buyers from different countries.

Sustainable Fashion

In recent years, there has been a growing emphasis on sustainable and eco-friendly fashion practices in Cairo. Some designers focus on using locally sourced and organic materials to create environmentally conscious clothing.

Cairo's Coffee Culture

Cairo's coffee culture is an integral part of the city's social fabric, offering a delightful experience for locals and visitors alike. Coffee has a long history in Egypt, and Cairo's coffee shops, known as "ahwas," play a significant role in the daily life of its residents. Here are some key aspects of Cairo's coffee culture:

Shisha (Hookah)

Alongside coffee, ahwas also offer shisha, or hookah, which is a traditional water pipe used for smoking flavored tobacco. Smoking shisha while sipping coffee is a common pastime for many Egyptians, especially in the evenings.

Ahwas and Social Gathering

Ahwas are traditional coffee shops found throughout Cairo, often located in bustling neighborhoods and on street corners. These establishments serve as popular social hubs where people gather to relax, socialize, and engage in lively conversations.

Arabic Coffee

The traditional coffee served in Cairo's ahwas is known as Arabic coffee or "qahwa." It is a lightly roasted coffee, brewed with cardamom for a unique flavor and aroma. Arabic coffee is usually served in small cups accompanied by a glass of water to cleanse the palate.

Coffee Rituals

Coffee drinking in Cairo is often accompanied by social rituals, such as offering coffee to guests as a sign of hospitality. Serving coffee during family gatherings and special occasions is a common tradition.

Historic Coffeehouses

Cairo is home to some iconic historic coffeehouses that have been operating for centuries. These establishments are not only places to enjoy coffee but also cultural landmarks that have witnessed the city's history and transformations.

Coffee and Culture

Cairo's coffee culture goes beyond the beverages themselves; it also includes various art forms like poetry, music, storytelling, and board games. Coffeehouses have been traditional venues for cultural gatherings and performances.

Coffee Carts and Street Vendors

In addition to coffee shops, Cairo's streets are dotted with coffee carts and street vendors selling coffee, particularly during festivals and public events.

Coffee and Ramadan

During the holy month of Ramadan, coffee plays a significant role in the pre-dawn meal (suhoor) before fasting begins, as well as in the post-dusk meal (iftar) when Muslims break their fast.

Expanding Coffee Culture

While traditional ahwas continue to thrive, Cairo's coffee culture is also evolving to include modern cafes and specialty coffee shops, catering to a diverse range of tastes and preferences.

Cairo's Modern Art Scene

Cairo's modern art scene is a dynamic and thriving community that reflects the city's position as a cultural hub of the Middle East. The city has been a center for artistic expression and creativity, attracting artists from Egypt and beyond. Cairo's modern art scene encompasses a wide range of artistic styles, mediums, and themes, drawing inspiration from both traditional Egyptian heritage and contemporary global influences. Here are some key aspects of Cairo's modern art scene:

Contemporary Art Galleries

Cairo is home to numerous contemporary art galleries that showcase the works of emerging and established artists. These galleries provide a platform for artists to exhibit their creations and connect with art enthusiasts and collectors.

Art Festivals and Exhibitions

Cairo hosts various art festivals and exhibitions throughout the year, bringing together artists, curators, and art lovers. Events like the Cairo Art Fair and Cairo Biennale attract national and international attention, promoting the city's art and culture on a global scale.

Art Schools and Institutions

Cairo is home to prestigious art schools and institutions that foster the growth of young talents. The Cairo Opera House and the Faculty of Fine Arts at Cairo University are notable centers of artistic education and development.

Themes and Subjects

Cairo's modern artists explore a wide range of themes, including identity, social issues, political commentary, cultural heritage, and environmental concerns. Their works often reflect the complexities of modern Egyptian society.

Integration of Traditional Elements

Many modern artists in Cairo draw inspiration from Egypt's rich artistic and cultural heritage, incorporating traditional elements, motifs, and techniques into their contemporary works.

Public Art Installations

Cairo's public spaces feature various art installations, sculptures, and murals that add vibrancy and artistic flair to the city's urban landscape.

Street Art

Street art has become a prominent form of expression in Cairo, with talented artists using public walls and spaces to create thought-provoking and visually appealing artworks.

Cultural Exchange

Cairo's modern art scene actively engages in cultural exchange programs, collaborations, and residencies with international artists and institutions, fostering cross-cultural understanding and artistic dialogue.

Art Collectors and Patronage

The growing interest in contemporary art in Cairo has led to an increase in art collectors and patrons who support and promote local artists.

Digital Art and Technology

With the advent of technology, some artists in Cairo are exploring digital art, incorporating new media and innovative techniques into their creative processes.

Coptic Easter

Coptic Easter, also known as Pascha or Resurrection Sunday, is one of the most significant religious celebrations in the Coptic Christian calendar. The Coptic Orthodox Church, which follows the Julian calendar for its liturgical year, celebrates Easter on a different date than Western Christianity, which follows the Gregorian calendar. Coptic Easter typically falls on a date between early April and early May. Here are some key aspects of Coptic Easter:

Date

Coptic Easter is celebrated on the first Sunday following the first full moon after the vernal equinox. It can occur anywhere from April 4th to May 8th in the Gregorian calendar.

Lenten Period

The Coptic Easter season begins with a 55-day Lenten period known as the Great Lent or the Holy Lent. During this time, Coptic Christians observe fasting, prayer, repentance, and acts of charity.

Holy Week

The week leading up to Easter is known as Holy Week. It includes significant events such as Palm Sunday (commemorating Jesus' entry into Jerusalem), Holy Thursday (celebrating the Last Supper), Good Friday (commemorating the crucifixion of Jesus), and Holy Saturday (a day of prayer and anticipation).

Holy Saturday and Resurrection Service

On Holy Saturday evening, Coptic Christians attend the "Liturgy of the Light" service, which begins after sunset. During this service, the church is dark, symbolizing Jesus' burial. The priest lights a candle from the Holy Fire, and the light is passed from person to person until the entire church is illuminated. This represents the resurrection of Jesus Christ. The Resurrection service is a joyous celebration of Christ's triumph over death.

Easter Sunday

On Easter Sunday, Coptic Christians attend the joyful Easter liturgy. The service is filled with hymns, prayers, and readings from the Bible, celebrating the resurrection of Jesus Christ. It is a time of great rejoicing and spiritual renewal.

Traditions and Customs

During Coptic Easter, families gather for festive meals, exchange greetings of "Christ is Risen! Truly, He is Risen!" and engage in acts of charity and giving to the less fortunate.

Red Easter Eggs

Red eggs are an essential part of Coptic Easter symbolism. They represent the blood of Christ and the new life that comes through His resurrection. People exchange decorated red eggs as a sign of friendship and love.

Special Foods

Traditional Coptic Easter dishes include feseekh (fermented fish), which is a delicacy enjoyed during the Easter festivities.

Festivals and Celebrations

Cairo is a vibrant city that celebrates a variety of festivals and cultural events throughout the year. These festivals showcase the rich heritage, traditions, and religious significance of Egypt, providing both locals and visitors with opportunities to experience the city's lively spirit. Here are some of the major festivals and celebrations in Cairo:

Eid al-Fitr

This festival marks the end of Ramadan, the holy month of fasting for Muslims. Families gather to celebrate with feasts, prayers, and exchange of gifts.

Eid al-Adha

Also known as the Feast of Sacrifice, it commemorates Ibrahim's willingness to sacrifice his son in obedience to God. Muslims across Cairo perform special prayers and sacrifice animals, distributing the meat to those in need.

Coptic Christmas

Celebrated on January 7th, Coptic Christmas marks the birth of Jesus Christ. Festive liturgies and processions are held in churches across Cairo.

Easter

Coptic Easter follows the Orthodox Christian calendar and is celebrated with special religious services, candlelight processions, and family gatherings.

Cairo International Film Festival

As one of the oldest film festivals in the Middle East, the Cairo International Film Festival attracts filmmakers, actors, and cinephiles from around the world. The festival showcases a diverse selection of films and hosts special events and panel discussions.

Cairo Jazz Festival

This annual event celebrates jazz music and features performances by local and international jazz artists. The festival promotes cultural exchange and appreciation for this genre of music.

Cairo International Book Fair

Held in January/February, the Cairo International Book Fair is one of the largest book fairs in the Arab world. It attracts publishers, authors, and book enthusiasts from various countries, offering a diverse range of books and literary events.

Islamic New Year (Hijri New Year)

The Islamic New Year marks the beginning of the lunar Islamic calendar. It is observed with prayers, religious gatherings, and reflections on the significance of the new year.

Revolution Day (National Police Day)

Celebrated on January 25th, this public holiday marks the anniversary of the Egyptian Revolution of 2011. It is a day of commemoration and reflection on the country's history.

Sham el-Nessim

Celebrated on the Monday following Coptic Easter, Sham el-Nessim is an ancient Egyptian festival that welcomes the spring season. Families gather for picnics and enjoy traditional foods like salted fish and colored eggs.

Cairo International Music Festival

This music festival showcases a diverse range of musical genres and performers from Egypt and around the world. It celebrates the universal language of music and fosters cultural exchange.

Literature

Cairo has a rich literary tradition that spans thousands of years, making it a significant center for literature in the Arab world. Egyptian writers and poets have contributed immensely to the country's cultural heritage, producing works that reflect the complexities of Egyptian society, history, and identity. Here are some key aspects of literature in Cairo:

Ancient Egyptian Literature

Cairo's literary history dates back to ancient times when Egyptian scribes recorded religious texts, myths, historical records, and literary compositions on papyrus scrolls. The ancient Egyptian literature includes works like "The Book of the Dead" and the "Epic of Gilgamesh."

Arabic Literature

With the advent of Islam and the Arab conquest of Egypt in the 7th century, Arabic became the predominant language, and Cairo became a center for Arabic literature. Prominent scholars and writers emerged, and Cairo's libraries and educational institutions played crucial roles in preserving and disseminating Arabic literature.

Al-Azhar University

Established in the 10th century, Al-Azhar University in Cairo became a renowned center for Islamic studies and Arabic literature. It continues to be a leading institution for Islamic education and research.

Modern Egyptian Literature

Cairo's modern literary scene flourished in the 19th and 20th centuries with the emergence of prominent Egyptian writers, poets, and novelists. Prominent figures include Taha Hussein,

Naguib Mahfouz (Nobel laureate in Literature), and Yusuf Idris, among others.

Realism and Social Themes

Many Egyptian writers have focused on realism and social themes, portraying the everyday lives and struggles of ordinary Egyptians. Their works often touch on issues like social inequality, political activism, gender roles, and cultural identity.

Poetry and Prose

Cairo's literary tradition includes a rich heritage of poetry and prose. Poetry, in particular, holds a special place in Egyptian culture, with a long history of poetic expression in classical Arabic, colloquial Egyptian Arabic, and free verse.

Cairo International Book Fair

The Cairo International Book Fair is one of the largest and oldest book fairs in the Arab world, attracting publishers, authors, and book enthusiasts from various countries. It provides a platform for promoting literature and cultural exchange.

Contemporary Writers

Cairo continues to be a vibrant hub for contemporary writers and poets, with numerous literary events, book launches, and writing workshops held throughout the city.

Literary Cafés and Cultural Spaces

Cairo's literary culture is also evident in its numerous literary cafés and cultural spaces, where writers, intellectuals, and readers come together to discuss literature, art, and societal issues.

Islamic Ramadan

Islamic Ramadan, also known as the holy month of fasting, is one of the most significant and sacred periods in the Islamic calendar. It is observed by Muslims worldwide as a time of spiritual reflection, increased devotion, and self-discipline. Ramadan is the ninth month of the Islamic lunar calendar and holds immense religious and cultural importance. Here are some key aspects of Islamic Ramadan:

Fasting (Sawm)

The primary act of worship during Ramadan is fasting from dawn (Fajr) to sunset (Maghrib). Muslims abstain from food, drink, smoking, and marital relations during daylight hours. Fasting is an essential pillar of Islam and is observed as an act of obedience to Allah (God), self-purification, and empathy for the less fortunate.

Suhoor and Iftar

Muslims wake up before dawn to have a pre-fast meal known as Suhoor. The fast begins at Fajr prayer time. The fast is broken at sunset with a meal called Iftar, which is often started with the eating of dates and drinking water, followed by a larger meal.

Taraweeh Prayers

During Ramadan, Muslims perform additional night prayers known as Taraweeh after the Isha prayer. These prayers are conducted in congregation at mosques and are a time for spiritual reflection and seeking Allah's blessings.

Increased Acts of Worship

Muslims strive to engage in increased acts of worship during Ramadan, such as reading the Quran, performing voluntary prayers (Nafl), making extra supplications (Dua), and engaging in charitable deeds.

Charity (Zakat and Sadaqah)

Giving to those in need is highly encouraged during Ramadan. Muslims are urged to pay their annual obligatory charity (Zakat) and engage in voluntary acts of giving (Sadaqah) to help those less fortunate.

Night of Laylat al-Qadr

Also known as the Night of Decree or Power, Laylat al-Qadr is believed to be the night when the Quran was first revealed to the Prophet Muhammad by Allah. It is considered the most blessed night of the year, and Muslims seek its blessings through worship and prayer, particularly during the last ten nights of Ramadan.

Spiritual Reflection and Self-Purification

Ramadan is seen as a time for self-examination, increased devotion, and seeking forgiveness from Allah. Muslims strive to improve their character, strengthen their faith, and cultivate patience and gratitude.

Community and Family Bonding

Ramadan fosters a sense of community and family bonding. Muslims come together for communal prayers, Iftar meals, and charity events, strengthening their social ties and unity.

Fasting Exceptions

Certain groups are exempt from fasting during Ramadan, such as children, the elderly, pregnant or nursing women, travelers, and those with health conditions. They may make up the missed fasts later or provide food to the needy as expiation.

ACTIVITIES AND ADVENTURES

Cairo offers a wide range of activities and adventures that cater to different interests and preferences. Whether you're a history buff, an art enthusiast, an outdoor adventurer, or a food lover, Cairo has something to offer for everyone. Here are some exciting activities and adventures to experience in Cairo:

Sailing the Nile

Sailing the Nile River is a captivating and relaxing experience that allows you to soak in the scenic beauty and historical significance of Egypt's iconic waterway. The Nile has been the lifeblood of Egypt for thousands of years, and sailing on its waters offers a unique perspective on the country's rich history and culture. Here's what you can expect when sailing the Nile:

Felucca Sailing

Feluccas are traditional wooden sailboats that have been used on the Nile for centuries. These sailboats have triangular lateen sails and offer a leisurely and authentic way to cruise the river. Felucca rides are especially popular in Cairo, Luxor, and Aswan.

Nile Cruises

For a more luxurious and comprehensive Nile sailing experience, consider a Nile cruise. Nile cruises typically run between Luxor and Aswan, or vice versa, stopping at various historical sites and attractions along the way.

Serene Scenery

Sailing the Nile allows you to witness the serene and picturesque landscapes of Egypt. As you glide on the water, you'll see lush green riverbanks, palm trees, villages, and ancient ruins in the distance.

Historical Sites

Many of Egypt's most famous historical sites are located along the banks of the Nile. A Nile cruise offers the opportunity to visit iconic landmarks such as the Temples of Luxor and Karnak, the Valley of the Kings, the Temple of Kom Ombo, and the Temple of Philae, among others.

Sunset Views

The Nile's tranquil waters create the perfect setting for watching stunning sunsets. Whether you're on a felucca or a cruise ship, witnessing the sun setting over the river is a breathtaking experience.

Birdwatching

The Nile River and its surroundings are home to a variety of bird species. Keep an eye out for herons, kingfishers, ibises, and other birdlife as you sail along the water.

Nubian Culture

A Nile cruise that includes a visit to Aswan provides an opportunity to learn about the fascinating Nubian culture. Nubian villages along the riverbanks offer a glimpse into their unique traditions and customs.

Relaxation and Tranquility

Sailing on the Nile is a peaceful and tranquil experience. It's a chance to unwind, enjoy the gentle breeze, and escape the bustling city life.

Photography Opportunities

With its scenic beauty and historic sites, the Nile River offers excellent opportunities for photography. Capture stunning shots of temples, landscapes, and local life along the river.

Desert Adventures

Egypt's vast deserts offer a playground for thrilling desert adventures, providing visitors with a chance to explore the country's rugged and otherworldly landscapes. From camel trekking to sandboarding, there are numerous activities that cater to adventure seekers. Here are some exciting desert adventures to experience in Egypt:

Desert Safari

Embark on a desert safari in the Western Desert or the Sinai Peninsula. Ride in a 4x4 vehicle with experienced guides who will take you off the beaten path to explore remote areas and stunning desert landscapes.

Camel Trekking

Experience the traditional way of traversing the desert on a camel trek. Ride through sand dunes and vast expanses, just as caravans did centuries ago.

Sandboarding

Try sandboarding on the desert's golden dunes. Slide down the slopes on a sandboard for an adrenaline-pumping experience.

Stargazing

Egypt's deserts offer some of the best stargazing opportunities. Spend a night in the desert and marvel at the clear, starry skies away from city lights.

Desert Camping

Experience the magic of the desert by camping under the stars. Enjoy traditional Bedouin hospitality and cuisine during your camping adventure.

Hot Air Balloon Rides

Take a hot air balloon ride over the desert and witness the breathtaking landscapes from the sky.

Jeep Tours

Join a jeep tour and explore the desert's hidden gems, including oases, canyons, and unique rock formations.

Oasis Visits

Explore lush oases amid the barren desert. Visit places like Siwa Oasis and Bahariya Oasis, known for their natural beauty and ancient history.

Desert Hiking

Go on a desert hiking expedition and discover the diverse flora and fauna that have adapted to the harsh desert environment.

Desert Yoga and Meditation

Experience a peaceful and meditative retreat in the desert, practicing yoga and meditation surrounded by the tranquil desert scenery.

Desert Wildlife Watching

Keep an eye out for desert wildlife, such as desert foxes, ibex, and various bird species, during your desert adventures.

Quad Biking

For an exhilarating experience, try quad biking on the desert's sandy terrain.

Visiting Ancient Rock Art

Some areas in the desert are adorned with ancient rock art and petroglyphs, providing a glimpse into the region's rich history.

Day Trips from Cairo

Cairo's strategic location in Egypt's heart makes it a perfect starting point for various day trips to explore the country's rich history, culture, and natural beauty. Here are some fantastic day trips you can take from Cairo:

Giza Pyramids and Sphinx

Explore the iconic Pyramids of Giza and the Sphinx, located just a short distance from Cairo. Marvel at the ancient wonders and learn about Egypt's fascinating history.

Saqqara

Visit the Saqqara complex, which includes the Step Pyramid of Djoser, one of the earliest stone structures in the world, and various ancient tombs.

Memphis and Ramses II

Discover the ancient capital of Egypt, Memphis, with its fascinating archaeological remains and the colossal statue of Ramses II.

Dahshur

Explore the Dahshur necropolis, home to the Bent Pyramid and the Red Pyramid, two of Egypt's lesser-known but impressive pyramids.

Alexandria

Take a day trip to Alexandria, the historic coastal city, to visit the Citadel of Qaitbay, the Library of Alexandria, and Pompey's Pillar.

Luxor

Though it's a longer day trip, it's possible to fly to Luxor from Cairo and explore the famous temples and tombs of ancient Thebes, including the Karnak Temple, Valley of the Kings, and Hatshepsut's Temple.

Wadi Natrun

Journey to Wadi Natrun to visit the ancient Coptic monasteries in the desert.

Fayoum Oasis

Discover the serene Fayoum Oasis, known for its beautiful landscapes, Lake Qarun, and ancient sites like the Pyramid of Hawara and the Valley of the Whales.

Ras Muhammad National Park

If you're interested in diving or snorkeling, head to Ras Muhammad National Park at the tip of the Sinai Peninsula for vibrant coral reefs and marine life.

Sakkara Country Club

For a day of leisure, consider visiting Sakkara Country Club, which offers a range of activities such as swimming, horseback riding, and golf.

St. Catherine's Monastery

Take a day trip to St. Catherine's Monastery at the base of Mount Sinai, an important religious site for Christians and a great location for hiking enthusiasts.

Al-Fayyum Desert

Enjoy a desert adventure in Al-Fayyum, where you can go sandboarding, explore the desert landscapes, and visit the Magic Lake.

Cairo Citadel and Khan El-Khalili

Spend the day exploring Cairo's historical sites, including the Cairo Citadel and the famous Khan El-Khalili bazaar.

Shopping In Cairo

Cairo offers a vibrant and diverse shopping experience, catering to a wide range of tastes and budgets. From traditional bazaars and markets to modern shopping malls, the city provides ample opportunities for buying souvenirs, handicrafts, clothing, and more. Here are some of the best places for shopping in Cairo:

Khan El-Khalili

Khan El-Khalili is Cairo's most famous and historic bazaar, dating back to the 14th century. It is a bustling maze of narrow alleys and shops, offering everything from jewelry and textiles to spices, souvenirs, and traditional crafts. Bargaining is a common practice here, so be prepared to haggle for the best prices.

Old Cairo Souk

Located near the Khan El-Khalili, the Old Cairo Souk is a smaller and less touristy market that offers a more authentic local shopping experience. It's a great place to find antiques, textiles, and unique souvenirs.

Islamic Cairo's Street of the Tentmakers (Sharia Khayamiya)

This street is famous for its colorful and intricately embroidered textiles known as Khayamiya. You can find a wide range of textile products, including cushion covers, wall hangings, and bedspreads.

Bab El-Louk Market

Located in Downtown Cairo, this market is known for its affordable clothing, shoes, and accessories. It's a great place to shop for trendy items at budget-friendly prices.

Citystars Mall

Citystars is one of Cairo's largest and most popular shopping malls, offering a vast selection of international and local brands. It's a one-stop destination for fashion, electronics, entertainment, and dining.

Cairo Festival City Mall

Another modern shopping mall in Cairo, Cairo Festival City Mall, offers a luxurious shopping experience with high-end brands and designer boutiques.

Mall of Arabia

Situated on the outskirts of Cairo, Mall of Arabia is one of the city's largest malls, featuring a wide range of shops, restaurants, and entertainment facilities.

Souq El Gomaa (Friday Market)

This sprawling open-air market, held on Fridays, is a treasure trove for bargain hunters. You can find second-hand items, vintage goods, electronics, and more at affordable prices.

Wekalet El-Balah

This historical market in Islamic Cairo specializes in traditional Egyptian crafts, including handmade copperware, glassware, and wooden products.

Zamalek Boutiques

The upscale neighborhood of Zamalek is home to boutique shops and galleries, offering unique and stylish clothing, jewelry, and art.

Mohandiseen Boutiques

Mohandiseen is known for its fashion boutiques, offering a mix of local and international brands.

Egyptian Perfume Shops

Cairo has many perfume shops that sell traditional Egyptian fragrances and essential oils, such as those made from jasmine and sandalwood.

Crafts and Souvenir Shopping Adventure

Crafts and souvenir shopping in Cairo can be a delightful adventure, allowing you to discover the city's rich artistic heritage and take home unique and meaningful mementos of your trip. Here are some craft markets, shops, and souvenirs to explore during your shopping adventure in Cairo:

Khan El-Khalili

Start your adventure at Cairo's iconic Khan El-Khalili bazaar, where you'll find a vast array of crafts and souvenirs. Look for traditional Egyptian textiles, such as colorful scarves, embroidered cushion covers, and Bedouin-inspired rugs.

Islamic Cairo's Street of the Tentmakers (Sharia Khayamiya)

This street is renowned for its stunning Khayamiya textiles. These intricately embroidered fabrics make for unique and eye-catching souvenirs.

Wekalet El-Balah

Located in Islamic Cairo, this market is an excellent place to shop for Egyptian handicrafts, including hand-carved wooden items, copper and brass utensils, and blown glass products.

Egyptian Papyrus

Purchase authentic Egyptian papyrus paintings depicting ancient hieroglyphics, gods and goddesses, or scenes from daily life. Look for reputable shops to ensure the papyrus is genuine.

Perfumes and Essential Oils

Explore the perfume shops in Cairo to find traditional Egyptian fragrances made from natural ingredients like jasmine, rose, and sandalwood. These make for delightful and aromatic souvenirs.

Mother-of-Pearl Crafts

Look for intricate and beautiful mother-of-pearl inlaid boxes, picture frames, and mirrors that showcase the artistry of Egyptian craftsmen.

Alabaster Items

Egypt is known for its alabaster crafts. Purchase alabaster vases, candle holders, and sculptures, often found in various colors and sizes.

Gold and Silver Jewelry

Cairo's gold and silver markets offer an assortment of beautifully crafted jewelry inspired by Egyptian motifs and symbols.

Nubian Crafts

If you're interested in unique souvenirs, visit Nubian craft shops in Aswan or Cairo. Look for colorful textiles, pottery, and beaded jewelry made by Nubian artisans.

Cartouche

Get personalized cartouches, which are ornate nameplates with hieroglyphics spelling out your name in ancient Egyptian style.

Handmade Ceramics

Discover shops selling hand-painted ceramics with traditional Egyptian patterns and designs.

Spices and Teas

Pick up a variety of aromatic spices and traditional Egyptian teas to bring the flavors of Egypt home with you.

Explore Egyptian Hieroglyphics

Egyptian hieroglyphics are a fascinating and ancient writing system used by the ancient Egyptians to record their language and communicate their thoughts, beliefs, and history. The word "hieroglyphics" comes from the Greek words "hieros," meaning sacred, and "glyphein," meaning to carve. The Egyptians used this script in religious, ceremonial, and monumental contexts. Here's an exploration of Egyptian hieroglyphics:

Origins

Hieroglyphics emerged around 3000 BCE during the Early Dynastic Period. They evolved from earlier pictorial representations used for accounting and communication.

Writing System

Egyptian hieroglyphics combine logograms (word symbols), ideograms (concept symbols), and phonetic symbols (representing sounds). They were usually written from right to left or left to right, with some exceptions.

Components

Hieroglyphs can be divided into three main categories: phonograms (representing sounds), ideograms (representing ideas or concepts), and determinatives (signs that provide context to the preceding words).

Rosetta Stone

The decipherment of hieroglyphics was made possible through the discovery of the Rosetta Stone in 1799. The stone contains a decree written in three scripts: hieroglyphics, Demotic (a later Egyptian script), and Ancient Greek, which enabled scholars to decipher the hieroglyphics.

Scribes

Scribes were highly skilled individuals responsible for reading and writing hieroglyphics. They held prestigious positions in ancient Egyptian society.

Materials

Hieroglyphics were inscribed on various surfaces, including stone monuments, temple walls, papyrus scrolls, and wooden coffins.

Hieratic and Demotic Scripts

Hieroglyphics coexisted with two simplified scripts: Hieratic (a cursive version used for everyday writing) and Demotic (a later script used for legal and administrative documents).

Egyptian Hieroglyphic Alphabet

Unlike modern alphabets, Egyptian hieroglyphics did not have letters representing individual sounds. Instead, each hieroglyph represented either a specific word or an idea.

Pictorial Representations

Hieroglyphics often took the form of pictorial representations of objects, animals, and people. For example, the hieroglyph for "sun" was a circle with a dot in the center, representing the sun and its rays.

Hieroglyphic Numbers

Hieroglyphics were also used for numerical notations. For instance, a heel bone represented the number 1, a tadpole symbolized 100, and a lotus flower stood for 1,000.

Religious and Mythological Significance

Many hieroglyphics were associated with religious beliefs and mythology, depicting gods, goddesses, and important rituals.

Decline

The use of hieroglyphics declined after the Roman conquest of Egypt in 30 BCE. It gradually fell out of use in favor of the Greek-based Coptic script.

Quad Biking in the Desert

Quad biking in the desert is an exhilarating and adventurous activity that allows you to explore the vast and stunning desert landscapes of Egypt. The desert regions around Cairo, such as the Giza Pyramids area and the nearby deserts of the Sahara, provide perfect terrains for quad biking. Here's what you can expect from a quad biking experience in the desert:

Safety Briefing

Before starting the adventure, you'll receive a safety briefing from experienced guides who will explain how to operate the quad bikes safely.

Equipment

You'll be provided with all the necessary safety gear, including helmets and goggles, to ensure your safety during the ride.

Riding Instruction

If you're new to quad biking, the guides will give you basic riding instructions to help you feel more comfortable and confident on the quad bike.

Adventure in the Desert

Once you're ready, the real fun begins as you set off on your quad bike adventure through the desert. Feel the adrenaline rush as you speed across the sandy dunes and open spaces.

Stunning Scenery

The desert landscapes offer breathtaking views, including sand dunes, rocky terrains, and vast expanses of untouched wilderness. The golden hues of the desert create a magical setting, especially during sunrise or sunset.

Professional Guides

You'll be accompanied by experienced guides who know the desert terrain well and can take you on exciting routes, ensuring a safe and enjoyable experience.

Group or Private Tours

Quad biking tours are available in both group settings or private tours for a more personalized experience.

Sunrise or Sunset Rides

Some operators offer quad biking tours during sunrise or sunset, adding a touch of magic to your desert adventure.

Duration

The duration of the quad biking experience can vary depending on the tour you choose, ranging from a few hours to half a day.

Photography

Don't forget to bring your camera or smartphone to capture the stunning desert scenery and the thrill of your quad biking adventure.

Dress Appropriately

Wear comfortable clothing suitable for outdoor activities, including closed-toe shoes, and consider bringing a scarf to protect your face from the desert winds.

Respect for Nature

While enjoying your quad biking adventure, remember to respect the fragile desert environment and follow the guidelines set by the tour operators to preserve the natural beauty of the desert.

Shop at Khan El-Khalili

Shopping at Khan El-Khalili is an exciting and vibrant experience that allows you to immerse yourself in the traditional atmosphere of a bustling Egyptian bazaar. This historic market in Cairo has been a hub of commerce and cultural exchange for centuries, and it remains one of the most popular destinations for tourists and locals alike. Here's what you can expect and some tips for shopping at Khan El-Khalili:

Diverse Shopping

Khan El-Khalili offers a wide range of products, from traditional Egyptian crafts and souvenirs to spices, jewelry, textiles, and clothing. You can find intricately embroidered textiles, handcrafted jewelry, colorful ceramics, brassware, and more.

Local Crafts

Look for authentic Egyptian crafts made by local artisans. Handmade products often have a unique charm and tell a story of the rich cultural heritage of Egypt.

Tea and Coffee

It's a common practice for shopkeepers to offer complimentary tea or coffee to their customers as a gesture of hospitality. Don't hesitate to accept and enjoy the traditional Egyptian hospitality.

Explore the Alleys

Khan El-Khalili is a maze of narrow alleys and streets, each offering a different array of shops and products. Wander through the labyrinth to discover hidden treasures and unique finds.

Cultural Experience

Shopping at Khan El-Khalili is not just about purchasing souvenirs; it's also an opportunity to engage with local culture and interact with the friendly and welcoming shopkeepers.

Have Fun

Lastly, enjoy the lively and vibrant ambiance of Khan El-Khalili. Take in the sights, sounds, and scents of the bazaar, and savor the unique experience of shopping in this historic market.

Take a Hot Air Balloon Ride

Taking a hot air balloon ride in Egypt is a truly magical and unforgettable experience, offering a unique perspective of the country's iconic landmarks and natural beauty. Hot air balloon rides are particularly popular in Luxor and Aswan, where you can soar above ancient temples, tombs, and the beautiful Nile River. Here's what you can expect from a hot air balloon ride in Egypt:

Early Morning Adventure

Hot air balloon rides are typically scheduled early in the morning, just before sunrise. This timing allows you to witness the breathtaking sunrise over the Egyptian landscape and enjoy cooler temperatures for a comfortable flight.

Pre-Flight Briefing

Before the flight, you'll receive a safety briefing from your experienced pilot and crew. They will explain the basics of the ride, including safety protocols and what to expect during the flight.

Takeoff

Once the balloon is inflated, you'll climb into the basket, and the adventure begins. As the hot air fills the balloon, you'll gently lift off the ground, and the magical journey starts.

Bird's Eye View

The sensation of floating peacefully through the air is truly surreal. From the balloon's vantage point, you'll have a bird's eye view of the surrounding landscape, including ancient temples, lush fields, the flowing Nile River, and the desert dunes.

Temple and Tomb Sightseeing

In Luxor, a hot air balloon ride often takes you over the west bank of the Nile, where you can marvel at the temples of Luxor and Karnak, the Valley of the Kings, the Temple of Hatshepsut, and other archaeological wonders.

Aswan's Nubian Villages

In Aswan, you can enjoy a hot air balloon ride over the Nile River and the surrounding countryside, including glimpses of Nubian villages and lush farmlands.

Peaceful Serenity

The flight itself is tranquil and serene, with only the occasional sound of the burner filling the silence. It's an opportunity to feel one with nature and appreciate the beauty of Egypt from a different perspective.

Landing and Celebration

After about an hour of floating through the air, the pilot will guide the balloon to a gentle landing. Upon landing, there is often a traditional celebration with music and refreshments to mark the end of the flight.

Photography Opportunity

The hot air balloon ride offers fantastic photo opportunities. Capture the stunning landscapes, ancient monuments, and the beauty of the Nile River from above.

Attend a Sound and Light Show

Attending a Sound and Light Show is a captivating and immersive experience that brings ancient Egyptian history to life through a combination of lights, sounds, and narration. These shows are held at some of Egypt's most iconic archaeological sites, such as the Pyramids of Giza, the Temple of Karnak, and the Temple of Philae. Here's what you can expect from attending a Sound and Light Show:

Illumination of Monuments

The show takes place in the evening after sunset when the monuments are illuminated with colorful lights, creating a dramatic and enchanting ambiance.

Narration and Storytelling

Throughout the show, a narrator guides the audience through the history and myths associated with the site. The story is often presented as if the ancient monuments themselves are speaking, recounting the events and legends of the past.

Historical Content

The show provides historical context about the site's construction, the rulers who built it, and the significant events that took place there.

Multimedia Presentation

The use of lights, lasers, and projections on the monumental structures enhances the storytelling, creating a visually stunning presentation.

Music and Sound Effects

The show is accompanied by music and sound effects that add to the emotional impact of the narration and visuals.

Multilingual Shows

Sound and Light Shows are often presented in multiple languages, including English, French, German, Spanish, and others, to accommodate international visitors.

Duration

The duration of the show varies but usually lasts around 45 minutes to an hour.

Seasonal Timing

It's essential to check the schedule and timings of the Sound and Light Show in advance, as the starting times may vary depending on the season.

Unique Atmosphere

The combination of lights, storytelling, and the majestic monuments create a unique and awe-inspiring atmosphere that transports visitors back in time.

Accessibility

Some sites offer seating arrangements for the audience, making the experience comfortable for visitors of all ages.

Photography

Photography is typically allowed during the show, but be mindful of using flash or bright lights that could disrupt the experience for others.

Visit Old Cairo Gates

Exploring the gates of Old Cairo is a captivating journey through history and a chance to witness the remnants of the city's ancient fortifications. Old Cairo, also known as Coptic Cairo, is a neighborhood that houses many historical churches, synagogues, and mosques, as well as some of Cairo's well-preserved gates. These gates once formed part of the city's defensive walls and are a testament to its rich past. Here are some of the notable gates in Old Cairo that you can visit:

Bab Zuweila (Zuweila Gate)

Bab Zuweila is one of the most famous and well-preserved gates in Cairo. It was built in the 11th century during the Fatimid period and served as one of the main gates of the old city. Visitors can climb to the top of the gate to enjoy panoramic views of Old Cairo.

Bab al-Futuh (Gate of Conquests)

Bab al-Futuh is another impressive gate built during the Fatimid period in the 11th century. It is located near the northern edge of Old Cairo and features intricate architectural designs and beautiful decorations.

Bab al-Nasr (Gate of Victory)

Bab al-Nasr is the third main gate of Old Cairo and is also from the Fatimid era. It is situated on the northern side of the old city and showcases stunning Islamic architecture.

Bab al-Wazir (Gate of the Minister)

This gate was constructed in the 14th century and is located near the Church of St. Sergius and Bacchus. Although it is not as well-preserved as the other gates, it still offers a glimpse into Cairo's historical fortifications.

Bab Darb Qirmiz

This gate, located near the Coptic Museum, is a reminder of Cairo's medieval defensive walls.

Bab al-Khalq (Gate of the People)

While not in Old Cairo, Bab al-Khalq is another historic gate worth mentioning. It is located near the Citadel of Cairo and dates back to the 11th century.

Attend Sufi Dance Performance

Attending a Sufi dance performance in Cairo is a mesmerizing and spiritual experience that offers insight into the mystical world of Sufism, a mystical Islamic belief system. The Sufi dance, known as "Sama," is a devotional act performed by Sufi dervishes to achieve a state of spiritual ecstasy and closeness to God. Here's what you can expect from a Sufi dance performance in Cairo:

Venue

Sufi dance performances are often held in historic venues, such as mosques, cultural centers, or dedicated Sufi performance spaces. One of the most famous places to witness a Sufi dance performance in Cairo is the Al-Ghouri Complex in Islamic Cairo.

Whirling Dervishes

During the Sufi dance, the participants, known as "whirling dervishes," wear traditional white robes with wide skirts, symbolizing their spiritual journey towards enlightenment.

Symbolism

The Sufi dance is rich in symbolism. The circular movements of the dervishes represent the unity and oneness with the divine, while the raising of their arms signifies their connection between heaven and earth.

Spiritual Ecstasy

The repetitive and rhythmic music played during the performance, combined with the swirling movements of the dervishes, creates an ambiance of spiritual devotion. It is believed that the dancers enter a trance-like state during the performance, experiencing a connection with the divine.

Religious Chants

Live musicians and singers accompany the dance with religious chants and traditional Sufi music, enhancing the spiritual experience of the audience.

Cultural Experience

Attending a Sufi dance performance is not only a spiritual experience but also a cultural one. It provides insight into the rich heritage and traditions of Sufism in Egypt.

Respectful Attire

As the dance is a religious and spiritual event, it is essential to dress modestly and respectfully. Avoid revealing or inappropriate clothing out of respect for the sacred nature of the ceremony.

Photography and Etiquette

Some venues may allow photography during the performance, but it's essential to be discreet and respect the performers and other attendees. Silence and attentiveness during the performance are also customary.

Ticketing

It's advisable to check in advance if tickets are required to attend the Sufi dance performance and if there are specific dates and times for the shows.

Timings

The timing of Sufi dance performances can vary, so it's best to confirm the schedule in advance to ensure you don't miss the opportunity to witness this unique experience.

ANCIENT MONUMENTS

C airo, as the capital of Egypt, is home to numerous ancient monuments that showcase the rich history and civilization of the region. Here are some of the most prominent ancient monuments you can explore in and around Cairo:

Saqqara

Saqqara is an ancient archaeological site located about 30 kilometers (19 miles) south of Cairo, Egypt. It is one of the most significant and historically rich necropolises in Egypt and served as the burial ground for the ancient Egyptian capital of Memphis. Saqqara is renowned for its numerous pyramids, tombs, and funerary complexes, making it a must-visit destination for history enthusiasts. Here are some key highlights of Saqqara:

Step Pyramid of Djoser

The Step Pyramid of Djoser is the most famous and distinctive structure at Saqqara. It is considered the world's oldest stone-cut pyramid and was built during the Third Dynasty for Pharaoh Djoser. Designed by the architect Imhotep, the pyramid is a revolutionary architectural achievement that marked the transition from mastaba tombs to pyramids.

Mastaba Tombs

Saqqara is home to numerous mastaba tombs, which were rectangular structures built to house the remains of nobles and high-ranking officials. These tombs often had elaborate decorations and inscriptions.

Pyramid of Unas

The Pyramid of Unas is one of the smaller pyramids at Saqqara and was constructed for Pharaoh Unas during the Fifth Dynasty. It is famous for its pyramid texts, a collection of religious and funerary spells inscribed on the walls of the burial chamber.

Serapeum

The Serapeum is an underground complex that served as the burial place for the sacred Apis bulls, which were considered the incarnation of the god Ptah. The Serapeum contains a series of large granite sarcophagi where the mummified remains of the Apis bulls were interred.

Teti Pyramid Complex

The pyramid complex of Pharaoh Teti, the first ruler of the Sixth Dynasty, includes the Teti Pyramid, a mortuary temple, and various tombs. The pyramid's interior features beautiful pyramid texts.

Imhotep Museum

Opened in 2006, the Imhotep Museum at Saqqara displays artifacts and objects related to the site's history, including statues, tools, and archaeological findings.

Other Notable Tombs

Saqqara has many other tombs and burial sites, some of which are still being excavated and studied by archaeologists.

Memphis

Memphis, also known as "Ineb-Hedj," was an ancient city located near present-day Cairo, Egypt. It served as the capital of Egypt during different periods of its long history and was one of the most important cities in the ancient world. Today, the ruins of Memphis are part of the UNESCO World Heritage Site known as Memphis and its Necropolis - the Pyramid Fields from Giza to Dahshur. Here are some key points about ancient Memphis:

Historical Significance

Memphis was founded around 3100 BCE and was the capital of Egypt during the Old Kingdom and part of the Middle Kingdom. It served as a political, cultural, and religious center for centuries and was a significant hub for trade and commerce.

Location

The ancient city of Memphis was situated on the western bank of the Nile River, near the modern-day town of Mit Rahina.

Temples and Monuments

Memphis was home to numerous temples and monuments dedicated to various Egyptian deities and pharaohs. The Temple of Ptah, dedicated to the creator god Ptah, was the most prominent religious structure in the city.

The Great Colossus of Ramesses II

One of the most famous statues from ancient Memphis is the Great Colossus of Ramesses II. This enormous statue of Pharaoh Ramesses II was carved from a single block of limestone and once stood at the entrance of the Temple of Ptah.

Decline and Abandonment

Over the centuries, Memphis faced several challenges, including changes in political power and the shifting course of the Nile River. By the time of the New Kingdom, the capital had moved to Thebes (modern-day Luxor), and Memphis gradually declined in importance. The city was ultimately abandoned and fell into ruin.

Archaeological Discoveries

Excavations at the site of Memphis have revealed a wealth of ancient artifacts, statues, and monuments, providing valuable insights into ancient Egyptian history and culture.

Open-Air Museum

The ruins of Memphis are now an open-air museum, where visitors can explore the remains of the ancient city, including the Temple of Ptah and various statues and artifacts.

Dahshur

Dahshur is an ancient archaeological site located approximately 40 kilometers (25 miles) south of Cairo, Egypt. It is renowned for its well-preserved pyramids, which are some of the earliest examples of true pyramids built in ancient Egypt. Dahshur is a less-visited but equally significant site compared to the more famous Pyramids of Giza. Here are some key highlights of Dahshur:

Bent Pyramid

The Bent Pyramid is one of the most distinctive structures at Dahshur. It was built for Pharaoh Sneferu, the father of Khufu (builder of the Great Pyramid at Giza). The pyramid has a unique design, with a change in the angle of its slopes, giving it the appearance of being "bent." This change in angle was likely an engineering adjustment during construction to prevent structural instability.

Red Pyramid

The Red Pyramid is another important pyramid at Dahshur and is also attributed to Pharaoh Sneferu. It is the world's first successful smooth-sided pyramid, and it served as a model for the construction of the Great Pyramid at Giza. The pyramid gets its name from the reddish hue of its limestone casing stones.

Sneferu's Pyramid Complex

In addition to the Bent Pyramid and the Red Pyramid, Dahshur is home to various other structures, including satellite pyramids and a mortuary temple, all part of the pyramid complex built for Pharaoh Sneferu.

Pyramid of Amenemhat III

The Pyramid of Amenemhat III is from a later period, dating to the Middle Kingdom. It is a smaller pyramid compared to those of the Old Kingdom, and its exact purpose is still debated by scholars.

Archaeological Exploration

Dahshur has been the subject of extensive archaeological exploration and restoration efforts, providing valuable insights into the construction techniques and architectural evolution of Egyptian pyramids.

Fewer Crowds

Unlike the Pyramids of Giza, Dahshur receives fewer visitors, making it an excellent destination for travelers seeking a quieter and more intimate experience with ancient Egypt's monumental history.

Citadel of Salah El-Din

The Citadel of Salah El-Din, also known as the Citadel of Cairo or simply the Cairo Citadel, is a medieval Islamic fortress and historic site located on a prominent hill in Cairo, Egypt. It is one of the city's most iconic landmarks and a must-visit destination for travelers interested in Egypt's rich history and Islamic architecture. Here are some key highlights of the Citadel of Salah El-Din:

Historical Significance

The Citadel was constructed by the Ayyubid ruler Salah El-Din (Saladin) between 1176 and 1183 AD as a defense against the Crusaders. It served as the seat of power for many subsequent rulers of Egypt, including the Mamluks and Ottomans.

Architecture and Layout

The Citadel is an impressive example of Islamic military architecture, featuring massive stone walls, imposing gates, and numerous towers. Within the Citadel complex, you'll find several historic mosques, palaces, and museums.

Mosque of Sultan al-Nasir Muhammad

Another significant mosque within the Citadel is the Mosque of Sultan al-Nasir Muhammad, built during the 14th century. It features intricate mosaics and beautiful Islamic calligraphy.

National Military Museum

Located within the Citadel complex, the National Military Museum houses a vast collection of military artifacts, weapons, and memorabilia from various periods of Egyptian history.

Muhammad Ali Mosque (Alabaster Mosque)

The most famous mosque within the Citadel is the Muhammad Ali Mosque, also known as the Alabaster Mosque. It was built between 1828 and 1848 by Muhammad Ali Pasha, the Ottoman ruler of Egypt, and is an outstanding example of Ottoman architecture with a mix of Turkish and Egyptian design elements.

Panoramic Views

The Citadel's strategic location on a hill provides stunning panoramic views of Cairo and the surrounding areas, including the Pyramids of Giza on a clear day.

Cultural Events

The Citadel occasionally hosts cultural events, concerts, and festivals, offering visitors a chance to experience Egyptian arts and entertainment.

Mosque of Ibn Tulun

The Mosque of Ibn Tulun is one of the oldest and most historically significant mosques in Cairo, Egypt. Located in the Sayyida Zeinab neighborhood, it stands as a remarkable example of Islamic architecture and serves as a major tourist attraction and place of worship. Here are some key highlights of the Mosque of Ibn Tulun:

Historical Significance

The Mosque of Ibn Tulun was built in the 9th century AD during the reign of Ahmad ibn Tulun, the Abbasid governor of Egypt. It is one of the few remaining examples of the early Islamic period in Cairo and holds immense historical and cultural importance.

Architectural Style

The mosque is known for its unique and impressive architectural style, reflecting a blend of Abbasid, Fatimid, and Coptic elements. Its massive mudbrick walls, adorned with decorative brickwork and carved stucco, make it one of the most well-preserved examples of its era.

Minaret

The mosque's minaret is a distinct feature and one of the oldest surviving minarets in Cairo. It is characterized by its spiral exterior staircase, which visitors can climb to enjoy panoramic views of the city.

Open Courtyard

The mosque features a large open courtyard surrounded by covered arcades with pointed arches. The courtyard is paved with stone and is used for prayer and communal gatherings.

Prayer Hall

The prayer hall is spacious and features a central nave with a wooden mihrab (prayer niche) oriented towards Mecca. The hall is supported by marble columns, some of which were recycled from ancient Roman and Coptic structures.

Geometric Patterns

The mosque's interior is adorned with intricate geometric patterns and Quranic inscriptions, creating a beautiful and serene atmosphere.

Conservation and Restoration

Over the centuries, the mosque underwent several restoration projects to preserve its historical integrity and structural stability.

Open to Non-Muslim Visitors

The Mosque of Ibn Tulun is open to non-Muslim visitors, who can explore its architecture, learn about its history, and appreciate its cultural significance.

Coptic Cairo

Coptic Cairo, also known as Old Cairo or Masr al-Qadima in Arabic, is a historic neighborhood in Cairo, Egypt, known for its rich Christian heritage. It is one of the oldest parts of the city and is home to various ancient Coptic Christian churches, monasteries, and landmarks. Coptic Cairo offers a fascinating glimpse into Egypt's early Christian history and is a significant pilgrimage site for Coptic Christians. Here are some key highlights of Coptic Cairo:

History

Coptic Cairo has a history dating back to the early Christian era in Egypt, with some of its churches dating back to the 4th and 5th centuries AD. It was an important center of Christianity in the region and continues to be a vital religious and cultural hub for Coptic Christians.

Coptic Museum

The Coptic Museum, located in Coptic Cairo, houses an extensive collection of Coptic art, artifacts, manuscripts, textiles, and relics dating back to the early Christian period in Egypt. The museum offers insights into the rich artistic and religious heritage of the Coptic community.

Hanging Church (Saint Virgin Mary's Coptic Orthodox Church)

The Hanging Church is one of the most famous landmarks in Coptic Cairo. Its name comes from the fact that the church is built above the gatehouse of an ancient Roman fortress. It is one of the oldest churches in Egypt and an essential pilgrimage site for Coptic Christians.

Church of St. Sergius and Bacchus

This ancient church is believed to have been built on the site where the Holy Family (Mary, Joseph, and the baby Jesus) sought refuge during their flight into Egypt. It is a popular destination for both Christian pilgrims and history enthusiasts.

Ben Ezra Synagogue

While Coptic Cairo is primarily associated with Christianity, it is also home to the Ben Ezra Synagogue, an important Jewish place of worship. The synagogue is believed to have been established on the site where the baby Moses was found in a basket among the reeds of the Nile.

Amr Ibn al-As Mosque

The Amr Ibn al-As Mosque, located near Coptic Cairo, is one of the oldest mosques in Egypt and Africa. It was built in 642 AD and marks the place where the Arab commander Amr Ibn al-As established the first Muslim capital in Egypt.

Religious Harmony

Coptic Cairo is an excellent example of religious coexistence, with Christian and Islamic places of worship existing in close proximity, reflecting Egypt's long history of religious tolerance and diversity.

Al-Azhar Park

Al-Azhar Park is a beautiful and historic public park located in the heart of Cairo, Egypt. It is a popular recreational and cultural destination that offers a peaceful oasis amidst the bustling city. Al-Azhar Park is not only known for its lush greenery and stunning landscapes but also for its historical significance and stunning views of Cairo's skyline. Here are some key highlights of Al-Azhar Park:

History

Al-Azhar Park was developed on what was once a landfill site during the 12th-century Ayyubid period. The initiative to transform the area into a park was undertaken by the Aga Khan Trust for Culture, and the park was opened to the public in 2005.

Gardens and Landscapes

The park features beautifully landscaped gardens with a variety of trees, plants, and flowers. It is designed in the style of traditional Islamic gardens, with winding pathways, water features, and shaded areas.

Lake and Fountains

Al-Azhar Park has a large lake at its center, offering a serene setting for leisurely boat rides. The park also has several fountains that add to the beauty of the surroundings.

Panoramic Views

One of the main attractions of Al-Azhar Park is its elevated location, which provides stunning panoramic views of Cairo's historic landmarks, including the Citadel and the Mosque of Ibn Tulun.

Al-Azhar Mosque

The park is named after the nearby Al-Azhar Mosque, one of the oldest and most prominent Islamic institutions in the world. The mosque is an important center of learning and is highly revered by Muslims.

Cultural Events

Al-Azhar Park often hosts cultural events, concerts, and festivals, making it a lively venue for various artistic and cultural activities.

Restaurants and Cafes

The park is home to several restaurants and cafes where visitors can enjoy traditional Egyptian cuisine and refreshing beverages while taking in the park's tranquil ambiance.

Community Impact

In addition to its recreational value, Al-Azhar Park has had a positive impact on the surrounding community. The park's development has led to improved living conditions for residents in the nearby historic neighborhood of Darb al-Ahmar.

Conservation and Sustainability

The park is a prime example of sustainable urban development, as it incorporates eco-friendly features, water recycling systems, and measures to preserve the environment.

PYRAMIDS OF GIZA

T he Pyramids of Giza are undoubtedly one of the most iconic and awe-inspiring ancient monuments in the world. Located on the Giza Plateau, just outside Cairo, Egypt, they have stood the test of time for over 4,500 years and continue to captivate the imagination of millions of visitors each year. Here's what you need to know about the Pyramids of Giza:

Pyramid of Khafre

The Pyramid of Khafre, also known as the Pyramid of Chephren, is the second-largest pyramid on the Giza Plateau, located near Cairo, Egypt. It is one of the three main pyramids at Giza and is closely associated with Pharaoh Khafre (Chephren), who ruled during the Fourth Dynasty of the Old Kingdom, around 2570–2544 BCE. Here are some key highlights and facts about the Pyramid of Khafre:

Size and Proportions

The Pyramid of Khafre stands at a height of approximately 136.4 meters (447 feet), making it slightly shorter than the Great Pyramid of Khufu. However, due to its higher elevation on bedrock, it appears taller than the Great Pyramid when viewed from certain angles. Its base measures around 215.5 meters (706 feet) on each side.

Construction

Like the other pyramids at Giza, the Pyramid of Khafre was constructed using large limestone blocks quarried from nearby areas. The blocks were then carefully placed to form the pyramid's smooth sides, although much of the outer casing stones have eroded or been removed over the centuries.

Mortuary Temple

The Pyramid of Khafre was part of a larger funerary complex that included a mortuary temple on the east side. The temple served as a place for performing rituals and offering offerings to the deceased pharaoh's spirit.

Sphinx Connection

The Pyramid of Khafre is closely associated with the Great Sphinx, as they are both part of the same complex. The Sphinx, a mythical creature with the body of a lion and the head of a human, is located in front of the Pyramid of Khafre.

Burial Chamber

The interior of the Pyramid of Khafre contains a burial chamber where the pharaoh's sarcophagus was placed. The chamber's ceiling is made of massive granite blocks, and the walls are adorned with hieroglyphic inscriptions and religious texts.

Tomb Robbery

When the pyramid was first opened by explorers, it was found empty of its original burial treasures, as it had likely been plundered by tomb robbers in antiquity.

Valley Temple and Causeway

The pyramid complex also included a Valley Temple and a causeway that connected the pyramid to the Nile River. The Valley Temple was used for the mummification process and as a place to prepare the pharaoh's body for burial.

Tourist Attraction

The Pyramid of Khafre, along with the other pyramids at Giza and the Great Sphinx, is one of the most popular tourist attractions in Egypt, drawing visitors from around the world to marvel at its grandeur and historical significance.

Pyramid of Khufu (Great Pyramid)

The Pyramid of Khufu, also known as the Great Pyramid, is the largest and most famous pyramid in Egypt, located on the Giza Plateau, just outside Cairo. It is one of the Seven Wonders of the Ancient World and is one of the most significant architectural achievements in human history. Here are some key highlights and facts about the Pyramid of Khufu:

Pharaoh Khufu

The Great Pyramid was built during the reign of Pharaoh Khufu (also known as Cheops) of the Fourth Dynasty of the Old Kingdom, around 2580–2560 BCE. It was constructed as his tomb and is part of a larger funerary complex that includes smaller pyramids for his queens and mortuary temples.

Size and Dimensions

The Great Pyramid originally stood at a height of approximately 146.6 meters (481 feet), but erosion and the removal of its outer casing stones have reduced its height to about 138.8 meters (455 feet). The base of the pyramid covers an area of around 5.3 hectares (13.1 acres).

Construction

The construction of the Great Pyramid is a remarkable feat of engineering and architecture. It is estimated to have been built using around 2.3 million limestone blocks, with each block weighing several tons. The precise methods of construction are still the subject of debate among archaeologists and researchers.

Alignment

The Great Pyramid is precisely aligned with the cardinal points (north, south, east, west), demonstrating the ancient Egyptians' advanced knowledge of astronomy and mathematics.

Interior

The pyramid's interior consists of a series of corridors, chambers, and galleries. The main chamber, known as the King's Chamber, houses an empty granite sarcophagus, and the Queen's Chamber is located at a higher level.

Giza Complex

The Great Pyramid is part of the Giza Pyramid Complex, which also includes the Pyramid of Khafre, the Pyramid of Menkaure, the Great Sphinx, and various smaller pyramids and tombs.

Tomb Robberies

Despite its massive size and complexity, the Great Pyramid has been subject to tomb robberies throughout history. When it was first opened by Arab caliph Al-Ma'mun in the 9th century, the pyramid was found empty of its original burial treasures.

Symbolism

The pyramid is a symbol of the pharaoh's divine power and eternal rule, representing a stairway to the afterlife and the heavens.

Tourist Attraction

The Great Pyramid is one of the most visited and studied monuments in the world, drawing millions of tourists and researchers each year who come to marvel at its grandeur and learn about ancient Egyptian history and culture.

The Great Sphinx of Giza

The Great Sphinx of Giza is a magnificent and iconic limestone statue located on the Giza Plateau, just outside Cairo, Egypt. It is one of the most recognizable and enduring symbols of ancient Egypt and remains a source of fascination and mystery to visitors from around the world. Here are some key highlights and facts about the Great Sphinx:

History

The Great Sphinx is believed to have been built during the reign of Pharaoh Khafre (also known as Chephren) in the Old Kingdom, around 2500 BCE. It is carved out of a single piece of limestone and stands in front of the Pyramid of Khafre, one of the three Pyramids of Giza.

Symbolism

The Great Sphinx is a mythical creature with the body of a lion and the head of a human, generally believed to represent the pharaoh's divine power and authority. It is a guardian statue that was placed at the entrance to the Giza necropolis, serving as a protector of the pyramids and the souls of the deceased pharaohs.

Size

The Great Sphinx is an awe-inspiring statue with impressive dimensions. It stands about 20 meters (66 feet) tall, 73.5 meters (241 feet) long, and 19.3 meters (63 feet) wide. The face alone measures around 5.5 meters (18 feet) in height.

Missing Nose

One of the most enduring mysteries surrounding the Great Sphinx is the missing nose. The nose of the Sphinx is believed to have been broken off either due to natural erosion over the millennia or possibly during an act of vandalism by Napoleon Bonaparte's soldiers in the early 19th century.

Restoration

The Great Sphinx has undergone various restoration and conservation efforts over the centuries to preserve its structural integrity and protect it from further erosion.

Alignment

The Sphinx is precisely aligned to face the rising sun on the vernal equinox, which adds to its mystical significance and suggests an astronomical connection in its original purpose.

Archaeological Discoveries

Archaeologists and researchers continue to study the Great Sphinx to unlock its secrets and understand more about its construction and historical context.

Tourist Attraction

The Great Sphinx of Giza is one of the most visited tourist attractions in Egypt, attracting millions of visitors every year who come to marvel at its colossal size and gaze upon its enigmatic face.

Pyramid of Menkaure

The Pyramid of Menkaure, also known as the Pyramid of Mykerinos, is the smallest of the three main pyramids on the Giza Plateau, located near Cairo, Egypt. It is part of the Giza Pyramid Complex, along with the larger Pyramids of Khufu and Khafre. The Pyramid of Menkaure was built for Pharaoh Menkaure, also known as Mykerinos, who ruled during the Fourth Dynasty of the Old Kingdom, around 2532–2504 BCE. Here are some key highlights and facts about the Pyramid of Menkaure:

Size and Dimensions

The Pyramid of Menkaure has a height of approximately 66.5 meters (218 feet) and a base measuring around 105.1 meters (345 feet) on each side. While smaller in comparison to the other pyramids at Giza, it is still an impressive monument in its own right.

Construction

Like the other pyramids at Giza, the Pyramid of Menkaure was constructed using large limestone blocks, but it is notable for having a lower core made of rough stones. The outer casing stones, which would have given the pyramid a smooth appearance, have largely eroded or were removed over the centuries.

Mortuary Temple and Valley Temple

The pyramid complex included a mortuary temple on the east side of the pyramid and a Valley Temple located near the Nile

River. The mortuary temple served as a place for performing rituals and offerings to the deceased pharaoh's spirit, while the Valley Temple was used for the mummification process and as a place to prepare the pharaoh's body for burial.

Burial Chamber

The interior of the Pyramid of Menkaure contains a burial chamber where the pharaoh's sarcophagus was placed. The burial chamber has a simple design compared to the other pyramids, and it is made of red granite.

Queen's Pyramids

On the south side of the Pyramid of Menkaure are three smaller pyramids, believed to be the tombs of Menkaure's queens. These smaller pyramids are also made of limestone and have a stepped design.

Tomb Robbery

Like the other pyramids, the Pyramid of Menkaure was likely plundered by tomb robbers in antiquity, and its original burial treasures are no longer present.

Tourist Attraction

The Pyramid of Menkaure, along with the other pyramids and the Great Sphinx at Giza, is a popular tourist destination, allowing visitors to explore the ancient wonders of Egypt and learn about its rich history and culture.

MUSEUMS IN CAIRO

airo is a city rich in history and culture, and it is home to numerous museums that offer a fascinating insight into Egypt's ancient past, Islamic heritage, and modern art. Here are some of the most notable museums in Cairo:

Solar Boat Museum

The Solar Boat Museum is an archaeological museum located near the Great Pyramid of Khufu on the Giza Plateau, Egypt.

It houses one of the most remarkable discoveries related to ancient Egyptian funerary practices - the reconstructed Solar Boat of Khufu. Here are some key highlights and facts about the Solar Boat Museum:

Discovery

In 1954, while excavating around the Great Pyramid, archaeologist Kamal el-Mallakh discovered a disassembled boat buried in a pit on the south side of the pyramid. The boat was found in remarkable condition, with its wooden parts still intact.

Solar Boat

The boat discovered is often referred to as the "Solar Boat of Khufu" or the "Khufu Ship." It is an ancient ceremonial boat believed to be used for religious rituals and funerary processions. It was buried near the pyramid to accompany Pharaoh Khufu in the afterlife.

Reconstruction

The Solar Boat was carefully disassembled and transported to a specially built museum on the Giza Plateau, where it underwent a meticulous restoration process that took several years. The restoration team reassembled the boat using the original timbers, and the completed boat is now on display inside the museum.

Construction and Design

The Solar Boat is a wooden vessel with intricate designs and sophisticated craftsmanship. It is made of Lebanese cedarwood and is around 43.6 meters (143 feet) long, with a beam of around 5.9 meters (19 feet).

Purpose

The purpose of the Solar Boat is still a subject of debate among scholars. Some theories suggest that it might have been used for religious rituals associated with the sun god Ra or that it was intended to carry the soul of the deceased pharaoh across the sky with the sun god during the journey to the afterlife.

Solar Boat Museum

The Solar Boat Museum was constructed to house the reconstructed Solar Boat. It provides visitors with an opportunity to view the boat up close and learn about its history and significance in ancient Egyptian culture.

Importance

The Solar Boat of Khufu is one of the most important discoveries related to the funerary practices of ancient Egypt. It provides valuable insights into the beliefs and rituals surrounding death and the afterlife during the Old Kingdom.

Visitor Experience

Visitors to the Solar Boat Museum can admire the impressive craftsmanship of the ancient boat and gain a deeper understanding of the significance of boats in ancient Egyptian culture and religious beliefs.

Egyptian Museum (Museum of Egyptian Antiquities)

The Egyptian Museum, also known as the Museum of Egyptian Antiquities, is one of the most famous and significant museums in the world. It is located in Cairo, Egypt, near Tahrir Square, and it houses an extensive and diverse collection of artifacts from ancient Egypt. The museum is a treasure trove of historical, artistic, and archaeological wonders, offering visitors a comprehensive understanding of Egypt's rich and fascinating history. Here are some key highlights and facts about the Egyptian Museum:

History

The Egyptian Museum was established in 1902 by the French Egyptologist Auguste Mariette, who sought to create a centralized repository for the country's ancient artifacts. The museum's current building was constructed in 1900 and has since been expanded and renovated to accommodate its growing collection.

Collection

The museum's collection is vast, with over 120,000 artifacts spanning more than 5,000 years of Egyptian history. It includes statues, mummies, sarcophagi, jewelry, papyrus scrolls, pottery, funerary objects, and much more.

Tutankhamun's Treasures

One of the most popular attractions in the Egyptian Museum is the collection of treasures from the tomb of Tutankhamun, the young pharaoh who ruled during the New Kingdom. The collection includes his iconic funerary mask, golden coffins, chariots, jewelry, and other personal belongings.

Mummies

The museum is home to an impressive collection of royal mummies, including those of famous pharaohs such as Ramses II and Hatshepsut. Visitors have the opportunity to see these well-preserved ancient remains up close.

Royal Gallery

The Royal Gallery houses colossal statues and artifacts from the temples of various pharaohs, offering a glimpse into the grandeur and opulence of ancient Egyptian rulers.

Narmer Palette

The museum houses the Narmer Palette, a significant artifact from the Predynastic Period that commemorates the unification of Upper and Lower Egypt under King Narmer.

Rosetta Stone

While not part of the museum's collection, the famous Rosetta Stone, which played a crucial role in deciphering Egyptian hieroglyphics, was originally housed in the Egyptian Museum before being moved to the British Museum in London.

Future Relocation

The Egyptian government has planned to relocate the majority of the museum's collection to the Grand Egyptian Museum (GEM) near the Giza Pyramids. The GEM is intended to become the new flagship museum of Egyptian antiquities.

Visitor Experience

Exploring the Egyptian Museum offers a unique opportunity to immerse oneself in the splendor of ancient Egypt and witness artifacts that were created thousands of years ago.

Grand Egyptian Museum (GEM)

The Grand Egyptian Museum (GEM) is a massive archaeological museum located near the Giza Pyramids in Cairo, Egypt. It is one of the most ambitious and significant museum projects in the world, designed to be the largest museum dedicated to ancient Egyptian history and antiquities. The GEM is intended to house an extensive collection of artifacts, including those from the Old Kingdom, as well as the treasures of Tutankhamun. Here are some key highlights and facts about the Grand Egyptian Museum:

Location

The Grand Egyptian Museum is situated on a 50-hectare site, approximately two kilometers southwest of the Giza Pyramids. Its strategic location provides visitors with stunning panoramic views of the pyramids.

Purpose

The primary goal of the GEM is to preserve, display, and protect Egypt's vast collection of ancient artifacts while also offering an immersive and educational experience to visitors.

Collection

The museum's collection is vast and diverse, including over 100,000 artifacts spanning Egypt's long history, from prehistoric times to the Greco-Roman period. The highlight of the museum will be the complete collection of Tutankhamun's treasures, which will be displayed together for the first time.

Tutankhamun's Collection

The GEM will showcase approximately 5,000 artifacts from the tomb of Tutankhamun, making it the most extensive and comprehensive exhibition of the young pharaoh's treasures ever assembled.

Conservation and Restoration

The museum has state-of-the-art conservation and restoration labs where experts work to preserve and restore ancient artifacts, ensuring their longevity and maintaining their cultural value.

Architecture

The architecture of the GEM is awe-inspiring, with a stunning modern design that pays tribute to ancient Egyptian architectural elements. The museum's main entrance is an enormous glass-fronted edifice, offering an imposing and grand welcome to visitors.

Education and Research

The Grand Egyptian Museum aims to be a center for educational and research activities, providing scholars and researchers with access to its vast collection for further study and exploration.

Sustainability

The GEM is designed to be an environmentally friendly and sustainable museum, incorporating various green building practices to reduce its ecological impact.

Opening Date

The opening of the Grand Egyptian Museum has been highly anticipated, and its official inauguration has been delayed multiple times. The museum was not yet open to the public. However, it is advisable to check for the latest information regarding its opening status and visiting hours.

Museum of Islamic Art

The Museum of Islamic Art is one of the most important museums in Cairo, Egypt, dedicated to showcasing the artistic and cultural heritage of the Islamic world. It is located in the historic district of Bab Al-Khalq and houses an extensive collection of Islamic art and artifacts from various periods and regions. Here are some key highlights and facts about the Museum of Islamic Art:

History

The museum was founded in 1881 and is one of the oldest and most significant Islamic art museums in the world. It was established during the reign of Khedive Ismail Pasha and was initially housed in the Al-Hakim Mosque before being moved to its current location in Bab Al-Khalq.

Collection

The Museum of Islamic Art boasts a vast collection of over 100,000 artifacts, including textiles, ceramics, metalwork, woodwork, glassware, calligraphy, manuscripts, and other decorative arts from various periods of Islamic history.

Architectural Design

The museum building itself is an architectural masterpiece, designed in a neo-Mamluk style, reminiscent of traditional Islamic architecture. It features beautiful arches, domes, and intricate geometric patterns, creating a harmonious ambiance that complements the exhibited artifacts.

Chronological Range

The museum's collection covers over 1,400 years of Islamic history, ranging from the 7th to the 19th century. It showcases the cultural diversity and artistic achievements of different Islamic dynasties and regions.

Thematic Sections

The museum's artifacts are displayed thematically, allowing visitors to explore various aspects of Islamic art, including religious artifacts, daily life objects, and items related to science, astronomy, and calligraphy.

Manuscript Collection

The museum houses an exceptional collection of Islamic manuscripts, including copies of the Quran, religious texts, and literary works, beautifully illustrated and calligraphed by skilled artists.

Restoration and Conservation

The Museum of Islamic Art has dedicated conservation and restoration departments that work tirelessly to preserve and maintain the delicate artifacts in the collection.

Educational Programs

The museum offers educational programs, workshops, and lectures, aimed at promoting a deeper understanding and appreciation of Islamic art and culture.

Tourist Attraction

The Museum of Islamic Art is a popular tourist destination in Cairo, attracting visitors from around the world who are interested in exploring the artistic and cultural heritage of the Islamic world.

Coptic Museum

The Coptic Museum is a fascinating cultural institution in Cairo, Egypt, dedicated to preserving and showcasing the rich heritage of Egypt's Coptic Christian community. It is one of the oldest museums in the country and is entirely devoted to Coptic art and artifacts. Here are some key highlights and facts about the Coptic Museum:

History

The Coptic Museum was established in 1908 and is located in the Old Cairo district, adjacent to the Babylon Fortress and the Hanging Church (Saint Virgin Mary's Coptic Orthodox Church). The museum's location is significant as it is in the heart of Coptic Cairo, an area with a long history of Coptic Christian presence.

Collection

The museum houses an extensive collection of over 16,000 artifacts, making it one of the largest collections of Coptic art and artifacts in the world. The exhibits include textiles, manuscripts, metalwork, woodwork, pottery, icons, frescoes, and other religious and secular objects dating back to early Christian and Byzantine periods.

Coptic Art

The museum's collection of Coptic art represents a unique blend of Egyptian, Roman, Byzantine, and Hellenistic artistic traditions, reflecting the cultural fusion of the region during the early Christian era.

Thematic Displays

The artifacts in the Coptic Museum are organized thematically and chronologically, providing visitors with a comprehensive understanding of Coptic art and culture through different historical periods.

Manuscript Collection

The museum's manuscript collection is particularly noteworthy and includes beautifully illuminated manuscripts with religious texts and illustrations.

Textile Art

The Coptic Museum is renowned for its remarkable collection of Coptic textiles, including intricately woven fabrics, tapestries, and garments adorned with colorful and symbolic designs.

Wooden Artifacts

The museum displays a range of wooden artifacts, such as intricately carved furniture, liturgical objects, and architectural elements from Coptic churches.

Icons and Religious Objects

The museum exhibits a rich assortment of Coptic icons, which are important religious artifacts in the Coptic Christian tradition.

Educational and Cultural Significance

The Coptic Museum plays a vital role in preserving and promoting Coptic heritage and culture. It offers visitors and scholars alike a chance to delve into the history, art, and religious practices of Egypt's Coptic Christian community.

Location

Being situated in Coptic Cairo, the Coptic Museum is surrounded by several important Coptic churches, monasteries, and historical sites, making it an ideal destination for those interested in exploring the Christian history of Egypt.

Museum of Modern Egyptian Art

The Museum of Modern Egyptian Art, located in Cairo, Egypt, is dedicated to showcasing and preserving the country's modern and contemporary artistic expressions. It is one of the leading art museums in Egypt, providing visitors with insights into the development of Egyptian art from the 19th century to the present day. Here are some key highlights and facts about the Museum of Modern Egyptian Art:

History

The museum was established in 1931 as the "Municipal Museum of Egyptian Modern Art" and was later renamed the "Museum of Modern Egyptian Art." It was founded by the pioneering Egyptian artist Mahmoud Mokhtar, who played a significant role in promoting modern Egyptian art.

Collection

The Museum of Modern Egyptian Art houses an impressive collection of modern and contemporary artworks, including paintings, sculptures, drawings, prints, photography, and mixed-media installations. The collection showcases the works of prominent Egyptian artists from various artistic movements and periods.

Exhibitions

The museum hosts rotating exhibitions that feature the works of both established and emerging Egyptian artists. It serves as a platform for contemporary artists to showcase their creations to a wider audience.

Egyptian Artistic Movements

The museum's collection represents various artistic movements that emerged in Egypt over the years, including the Art and Liberty Group (1938-1948), the Contemporary Art Group (1946-1950s), and the Contemporary Art Group (1950s-1960s), among others.

Mahmoud Mokhtar Gallery

The museum has a dedicated gallery named after the renowned Egyptian sculptor Mahmoud Mokhtar. The gallery displays some of his significant works, celebrating his contribution to modern Egyptian sculpture.

Influence on Egyptian Art

The Museum of Modern Egyptian Art has played a crucial role in shaping the trajectory of modern and contemporary art in Egypt. It has provided artists with a platform to experiment, innovate, and explore new artistic styles.

Cultural Center

Beyond exhibiting artworks, the museum serves as an essential cultural center that hosts lectures, workshops, and educational programs to engage the public and foster a deeper appreciation of Egyptian art.

Location

The museum is located in Cairo's Gezira district, near the Cairo Opera House and the Cairo Tower, making it easily accessible to both locals and tourists.

Recognition

The Museum of Modern Egyptian Art is a testament to Egypt's vibrant and evolving art scene, and it stands as a cultural landmark representing the country's contemporary creative spirit.

Museum of Civilization (Maspero Museum)

The Museum of Civilization, also known as the Maspero Museum, is an important archaeological museum in Cairo, Egypt. It is dedicated to showcasing the rich cultural heritage and history of Egypt from prehistoric times to the modern era. The museum houses a diverse collection of artifacts, including those from ancient Egypt, as well as objects representing various aspects of Egypt's social, cultural, and artistic development. Here are some key highlights and facts about the Museum of Civilization (Maspero Museum):

History

The museum was established in 1858 as part of the Egyptian Antiquities Service, and it was originally located in a building near the Cairo Citadel. In 1886, it was moved to its current location along the Nile River in the Maspero building, which was named after the French Egyptologist Gaston Maspero.

Relocation

There were plans to relocate the Museum of Civilization to the new Grand Egyptian Museum (GEM) near the Giza Pyramids. The move was part of an initiative to centralize Egypt's archaeological treasures and create a world-class cultural institution at the GEM.

Collection

The museum's collection covers a wide range of historical periods, from prehistoric times to the Islamic era. It includes artifacts from ancient Egypt, such as statues, pottery, jewelry, and mummies, as well as items representing various historical periods, such as artifacts from the Coptic and Islamic periods.

Thematic Displays

The museum's exhibits are organized thematically, allowing visitors to explore different aspects of Egypt's history, including its ancient civilizations, art and architecture, social life, religion, and technology.

Ancient Egyptian Artifacts

The museum showcases a selection of ancient Egyptian artifacts, providing insights into the daily life, religious beliefs, and artistic achievements of this ancient civilization.

Coptic and Islamic Art

The collection also includes significant artifacts from the Coptic Christian and Islamic periods, reflecting the cultural and religious diversity of Egypt over the centuries.

Educational Value

The Museum of Civilization serves as an important educational resource, offering visitors and researchers a chance to learn about Egypt's rich and diverse history and cultural heritage.

Cultural Significance

The museum contributes to the preservation and promotion of Egypt's cultural heritage, allowing both Egyptians and international visitors to appreciate the country's historical legacy.

Future Plans

With the planned relocation to the Grand Egyptian Museum, the Museum of Civilization (Maspero Museum) is expected to reach an even broader audience and continue to be a vital cultural institution in Egypt.

Manial Palace Museum

The Manial Palace Museum, also known as the Palace of Prince Muhammad Ali Tewfik, is a stunning historical palace located on Rhoda Island in the Nile River, Cairo, Egypt. It is a unique architectural gem and serves as a museum that offers visitors a glimpse into the opulent lifestyle of Egyptian royalty during the early 20th century. Here are some key highlights and facts about the Manial Palace Museum:

History

The palace was originally constructed between 1899 and 1929 as a residence for Prince Muhammad Ali Tewfik, the son of Khedive Tewfik Pasha, who was the ruler of Egypt during the late 19th and early 20th centuries.

Architectural Style

The Manial Palace is an exceptional example of Islamic architecture with influences from various architectural styles, including Ottoman, Moorish, Persian, and Fatimid. The palace's design combines traditional elements with modern features, creating a harmonious and aesthetically pleasing structure.

Scenic Location

The palace is situated on the Nile's eastern bank on Rhoda Island, providing visitors with beautiful views of the river and Cairo's skyline.

Palatial Complex

The Manial Palace is not just a single building but a vast complex that includes the palace itself, stunning gardens, courtyards, pavilions, and other ancillary buildings.

Art and Decorations

The palace interiors are adorned with exquisite decorations, including intricate woodwork, colorful ceramic tiles, stained glass windows, and elaborately designed ceilings. The lavish furnishings and art collection reflect the refined tastes of the royal family.

Gardens

The palace gardens are a true highlight, featuring a variety of trees, plants, and flowers from different parts of the world. The gardens are designed in a Persian style, with meandering pathways, fountains, and beautiful water features.

Museum Collection

The Manial Palace Museum houses an extensive collection of art, artifacts, and personal belongings of Prince Muhammad Ali Tewfik. The exhibits provide insights into the royal family's lifestyle, traditions, and historical context.

Public Opening

In 1955, the palace was converted into a museum and opened to the public, allowing visitors to explore its architectural beauty and experience the grandeur of Egyptian royalty.

Cultural Events

The Manial Palace Museum occasionally hosts cultural events, art exhibitions, and other activities that promote Egyptian heritage and arts.

Gayer-Anderson Museum

The Gayer-Anderson Museum, also known as Bayt al-Kiritliya, is a unique historical house museum located in Cairo, Egypt. It is named after its former owner, Major R.G.

Gayer-Anderson, an English military officer and Egyptologist who resided in the house during the first half of the 20th century. The museum showcases an impressive collection of art, artifacts, and furnishings, providing visitors with a glimpse into the life and tastes of an affluent 19th-century Egyptian family. Here are some key highlights and facts about the Gayer-Anderson Museum:

History

The Gayer-Anderson Museum is housed in two historic houses located in the heart of Islamic Cairo, adjacent to the famous Ibn Tulun Mosque. The houses were originally built in the 17th century, during the Mamluk period, and were later combined to create the unique residence that stands today.

Gayer-Anderson's Residence

Major R.G. Gayer-Anderson, a British officer and a passionate collector of art and antiquities, acquired the property in 1935. He lived in the house until 1942, during which time he restored and refurbished it, adding his extensive collection of Islamic art and furnishings.

Islamic Art Collection

The Gayer-Anderson Museum houses an exceptional collection of Islamic art and artifacts, including intricately carved wooden furniture, exquisite metalwork, pottery, textiles, and beautiful carpets.

Arabian Hall

The museum's Arabian Hall is one of its most remarkable features, with its richly decorated wooden ceiling, ornate mashrabiya (wooden latticework), and impressive collection of antique Persian and Syrian carpets.

Mashrabiya Balcony

The museum's balconies are adorned with intricate mashrabiya screens, providing stunning views of the surrounding Islamic Cairo neighborhood.

Decorated Rooms

The house features several rooms decorated in traditional Islamic and Ottoman styles, each with its own unique charm and artistic flair.

Courtyards

The museum's courtyards are beautifully landscaped and adorned with fountains, offering visitors a serene and relaxing atmosphere.

Filming Location

The Gayer-Anderson Museum has been used as a filming location for various movies and television shows, further enhancing its charm and historical significance.

UNESCO World Heritage Site

The Gayer-Anderson Museum is part of the Historic Cairo UNESCO World Heritage Site, along with the nearby Ibn Tulun Mosque and other historic landmarks.

Abdeen Palace Museum

The Abdeen Palace Museum, located in Cairo, Egypt, is a historic palace that served as the residence of Egypt's royal family during the late 19th and early 20th centuries. Today, it is a museum that showcases the rich history, art, and culture of Egypt's monarchy. Here are some key highlights and facts about the Abdeen Palace Museum:

History

The Abdeen Palace was originally built in 1863 by Khedive Ismail Pasha as a royal residence. It was named after the nearby Abdeen Square in Cairo. The palace underwent several expansions and renovations during the reigns of different Egyptian rulers.

Architectural Style

The palace is an impressive architectural masterpiece that combines neoclassical, rococo, and Islamic design elements. It features grand facades, beautiful gardens, and opulent interiors adorned with exquisite decorations.

Royal Residence

The Abdeen Palace served as the primary residence of Egypt's royal family during various periods, including King Fuad I, King Farouk, and later, President Gamal Abdel Nasser.

Museum Collection

In 1984, the palace was converted into a museum, opening its doors to the public and displaying a wide array of historical artifacts, including furniture, paintings, textiles, and personal belongings of the royal family.

The Silver Museum

Within the Abdeen Palace complex, there is a section known as the "Silver Museum," which houses a remarkable collection of decorative arts, including silverware, chinaware, and gifts presented to the royal family by foreign dignitaries.

Historical Significance

The Abdeen Palace is historically significant as it witnessed important events in Egypt's modern history, including the reigns of different rulers and the declaration of Egypt as an independent kingdom under King Fuad I in 1922.

Guided Tours

Visitors to the Abdeen Palace Museum can explore its grand rooms, halls, and gardens, and guided tours are available to provide insights into the palace's history and the lives of Egypt's royal family.

Cultural Events

The Abdeen Palace occasionally hosts cultural events, art exhibitions, and other activities that celebrate Egyptian heritage and arts.

Location

The Abdeen Palace is situated in central Cairo, making it easily accessible to both locals and tourists.

COPTIC ARCHITECTURE

C optic architecture is a unique style of architecture that developed in Egypt during the early Christian period, starting in the 4th century AD and continuing through the 7th century. It is closely associated with the Coptic Christian community in Egypt, which traces its roots back to the early days of Christianity. Coptic architecture is characterized by a fusion of ancient Egyptian, Roman, and Byzantine architectural elements, resulting in a distinctive and culturally rich architectural style. Here are some key features and characteristics of Coptic architecture:

Basilica and Church Layout

The basilica and church layout is a common architectural plan used in Christian churches, including many Coptic churches. The term "basilica" originally referred to a large public building in ancient Rome, but it was later adopted by the early Christians to describe a specific type of church layout. The basilica plan is characterized by a rectangular shape with a long nave (central hall) and one or more side aisles. Here are the key features of the basilica and church layout:

Nave

The central hall of the basilica is called the nave. It is typically the widest and tallest part of the church and extends from the entrance at one end to the apse at the other end. The nave is where the congregation gathers for worship.

Aisles

Flanking the nave on one or both sides are aisles, which are narrower and lower than the nave. Aisles provide additional space for movement, seating, or smaller chapels.

Apse

The apse is a semicircular or polygonal recess at the end of the nave, opposite the main entrance. It is usually where the altar is located and is considered the most sacred part of the church.

Transept (optional)

Some basilica-style churches include a transept, which is a cross-shaped section that intersects the nave and the aisles, forming a cruciform layout. The transept creates a cross-like shape when viewed from above.

Atrium (in some cases)

In some early Christian basilicas, an atrium, or enclosed courtyard, was located in front of the main entrance. The atrium served as a gathering space for the congregation before entering the church.

Columns and Arcades

Basilicas often have columns or piers that divide the nave from the aisles. Arcades, formed by the rows of columns, create visual and spatial separation between the central nave and the side aisles.

Roofing

The nave is usually covered with a higher and more prominent roof than the aisles, emphasizing its importance.

Windows and Lighting

Basilicas often have clerestory windows located at the top of the walls of the nave, allowing natural light to illuminate the central space.

Columns and Capitals

Columns and capitals are essential architectural elements found in various styles of architecture, including Coptic and other forms of Christian architecture. They play a crucial role in supporting the weight of the building and creating a visually appealing and decorative appearance. Here's an overview of columns and capitals:

Columns

Columns are vertical, cylindrical, or polygonal supports that typically stand upright to bear the weight of the structure above them, such as the roof or entablature.

They are placed at regular intervals along the sides of the nave and aisles in basilica-style churches, forming a colonnade that separates the central space from the side aisles.

In Coptic and Christian architecture, columns are often made of stone or brick, although other materials like wood may also be used. Various styles of columns exist, including Doric, Ionic, Corinthian, and composite, each with distinctive characteristics and proportions.

Capitals

The capital is the topmost part of a column and serves as a transition between the column and the load it supports. Capitals are highly decorative and provide an opportunity for artistic expression and architectural ornamentation.

In early Christian and Coptic architecture, capitals were often adorned with intricate carvings, including religious symbols, plants, animals, or human figures. The style of capitals can vary based on the architectural period, region, and cultural influences.

Arches and Domes

Arches and domes are architectural elements used in various styles of architecture, including Coptic and other forms of

Christian architecture. They serve both structural and decorative purposes, adding stability, visual appeal, and architectural grandeur to buildings. Here's an overview of arches and domes:

Arches

An arch is a curved structural element that spans an opening, such as a doorway or a window, and transfers the weight above it to its supporting columns or walls. Arches are fundamental to architectural engineering, as they distribute the weight of the building more efficiently than flat lintels or beams.

In Coptic and Christian architecture, you can find various types of arches, including semicircular arches (Roman arches), pointed arches (Gothic arches), and horseshoe arches (Moorish arches), depending on the architectural style and period.

Domes

A dome is a rounded vault or roof structure that forms an architectural hemispherical or onion-like shape. Domes are often used to cover large interior spaces, providing a sense of spaciousness and openness within a building.

In Christian architecture, domes are often found crowning the central space of a basilica or a church, such as above the crossing where the nave and transept intersect. Domes can be constructed using various materials, including stone, brick, concrete, or even glass, and they are often decorated with elaborate frescoes or mosaics on the interior surface.

Pendentives and Squinches

In some cases, to transition from a square or rectangular base to a circular dome, architectural features called pendentives or squinches are used.

Pendentives are triangular segments of a sphere that bridge the corners of a square or rectangular space to support the circular base of a dome.

Squinches are similar to pendentives but use a series of arches or corbeling to achieve the same effect, creating a polygonal base for the dome.

Both arches and domes are fundamental elements of Coptic and Christian architecture, and their use often reflects the technological and artistic achievements of their respective periods. These architectural features provide not only structural stability but also aesthetic beauty, enhancing the sense of sacredness and creating a visually impressive and uplifting environment for religious worship and spiritual contemplation.

Brick and Stone Construction

Brick and stone construction are two common building techniques used in various architectural styles, including Coptic and other forms of Christian architecture. Both materials have been employed throughout history for their durability, strength, and versatility in constructing various types of buildings. Here's an overview of brick and stone construction:

Brick Construction:

Bricks are rectangular blocks made of clay or clay-rich soil that are hardened by firing in a kiln or sun-dried, depending on the type of brick.

Brick construction is widely used for both structural and non-structural elements in buildings.

In Coptic and Christian architecture, bricks were often used for walls, arches, vaults, and domes, providing a cost-effective and durable building material. In some cases, bricks were left exposed as a design element, showcasing their natural color and texture.

Sun-dried mudbricks, known as adobe, were commonly used in early Coptic architecture and other ancient buildings due to their abundance and ease of production.

Stone Construction:

Stone is a natural building material extracted from quarries and used in various forms, such as blocks, slabs, and carved elements. Stone construction is considered more durable and long-lasting than brick construction, making it suitable for monumental and prestigious buildings.

In Coptic and Christian architecture, stone was often used for important architectural elements, such as columns, capitals, lintels, doorways, and facades. Stone was also used in construction for the facades of churches, monasteries, and other religious buildings, providing a sense of permanence and stability.

Combination of Brick and Stone:

Many Coptic and Christian buildings combine both brick and stone construction, using bricks for less visible or non-load-bearing elements and stone for more prominent and structurally significant parts. For example, while the walls may be constructed primarily with bricks, stone might be used for the columns, capitals, and decorative elements.

The use of brick and stone in Coptic and Christian architecture reflects the availability of local building materials and the technological capabilities of the time. Both materials contribute to the overall aesthetic and structural integrity of the buildings, making them enduring symbols of the cultural and architectural heritage of the region. Additionally, the skillful combination of brick and stone construction adds to the distinctive character and charm of Coptic and Christian architectural designs.

Coptic Cross

The Coptic Cross is a unique and significant symbol used in Coptic Christianity, an ancient Christian denomination with roots in Egypt. Also known as the Coptic Orthodox Cross, it holds deep religious and cultural meaning for the Coptic Christian community. The Coptic Cross is distinct from other Christian crosses and is recognizable by its particular design. Here are the key features and meanings of the Coptic Cross:

Shape

The Coptic Cross has a distinct shape that sets it apart from other Christian crosses. It consists of a simple Latin cross (a vertical line intersecting a shorter horizontal line) with an additional loop or circle at the top.

Ankh Symbol

The loop or circle at the top of the Coptic Cross resembles the ancient Egyptian hieroglyph known as the "ankh." The ankh is an ancient Egyptian symbol that represents life and eternal life, and its incorporation into the Christian cross symbolizes the eternal life through Christ.

Historical Significance

The use of the Coptic Cross dates back to the early days of Christianity in Egypt. It represents the rich cultural heritage of Coptic Christianity, which traces its origins to the apostolic era and has maintained its distinct traditions and liturgy.

Connection to Egyptian Heritage

The inclusion of the ankh symbol in the Coptic Cross is a unique way of connecting ancient Egyptian symbolism with the Christian faith. It signifies the continuity and transformation of religious beliefs in Egypt from the ancient past to Christianity.

Religious Symbolism

The vertical line of the cross represents the connection between heaven and earth, while the horizontal line symbolizes the connection between humanity and God. The loop at the top, resembling the ankh, emphasizes the theme of eternal life through Christ's sacrifice and resurrection.

Ornamentation and Decoration

The Coptic Cross may be decorated with various ornamental elements, such as intricate carvings, enamel work, or gemstones, reflecting the artistic traditions of Coptic craftsmanship.

Use in Religious Practices

The Coptic Cross is widely used in Coptic Christian churches, on altars, as jewelry, and in religious rituals and ceremonies.

Wall Paintings and Mosaics

Wall paintings and mosaics are important forms of artistic expression and decoration found in various styles of architecture, including Coptic and other forms of Christian architecture. Both techniques have been extensively used in churches, cathedrals, and religious buildings to convey religious themes, biblical stories, and sacred imagery. Here's an overview of wall paintings and mosaics:

Wall Paintings

Wall paintings, also known as frescoes, are paintings directly applied to the surface of a wall or ceiling while the plaster is still wet, allowing the paint to be absorbed into the plaster, creating a durable and long-lasting artwork.

In Coptic and Christian architecture, wall paintings are commonly found on the interior walls of churches, particularly in the apse, nave, and transept areas. Wall paintings often depict scenes from the Bible, the life of Jesus, the Virgin Mary, saints, and significant religious events. These paintings serve both an artistic and devotional purpose, visually narrating religious stories and providing a spiritual ambiance for worshippers.

Mosaics

Mosaics are artworks created by assembling small pieces of colored glass, stone, or other materials (called tesserae) to form a picture or design on a surface. Mosaics have been used in Christian architecture since early times, and they are known for their durability and ability to withstand the test of time.

In Coptic and Christian architecture, mosaics are often found on the walls, ceilings, and floors of churches and basilicas, adding splendor and beauty to the sacred spaces. Mosaic designs typically feature religious figures, symbols, and intricate geometric patterns.

Cloisters and Courtyards

Cloisters and courtyards are architectural features commonly found in Christian monasteries and religious buildings, including some Coptic churches. These spaces serve important functional and spiritual purposes, providing areas for contemplation, prayer, community gatherings, and recreation. Here's an overview of cloisters and courtyards:

Cloisters

Cloisters are covered walkways, typically surrounding a courtyard, with a series of arches or columns along one or more sides. They form an enclosed ambulatory, providing sheltered access to various parts of a monastery or religious complex. Cloisters are often found in Christian monastic communities, where they connect the church, chapels, refectory (dining hall), dormitories, and other essential areas used by the monks or nuns.

Courtyards

Courtyards are open outdoor spaces within a building complex, often enclosed by surrounding walls or buildings. Courtyards can be found in various types of architecture, including monasteries, palaces, and residential buildings, and they have been used since ancient times for a range of functions. In religious settings, courtyards often serve as a focal point for various activities, such as processions, ceremonies, and communal gatherings.

Defensive Architecture

Defensive architecture refers to the incorporation of various architectural features and elements designed to enhance the defensive capabilities of a building or structure. Such features were historically prevalent in many types of buildings, including castles, fortresses, city walls, and religious buildings, particularly during periods of conflict, instability, or vulnerability to external threats. Defensive architecture aimed to protect inhabitants, assets, and strategic locations from enemy attacks. Here are some key aspects of defensive architecture:

Fortifications

Fortifications are structures or walls built around a city, town, or building to protect it from invading forces. These walls often included battlements, crenellations, and watchtowers, allowing defenders to observe and repel attackers effectively.

Defensive Walls

Thick and robust walls were a common feature of defensive architecture. The thickness of the walls made it difficult for attackers to breach them, and the height provided an advantage for defenders to shoot arrows or throw projectiles at the enemy.

Moats and Ditches

Moats and ditches were dug around castles or fortifications to create a physical barrier, hindering direct access to the structure and requiring attackers to breach the moat before reaching the walls.

Drawbridges and Gatehouses

Drawbridges were a common feature of castles and fortifications. They were bridges that could be raised or lowered, providing a controlled entrance to the structure. Gatehouses served as additional defensive points with murder holes and arrow slits for defenders to repel attackers.

Bastions and Towers

Bastions and towers were projecting structures on the defensive walls, providing vantage points and allowing defenders to cover multiple angles of attack.

Defensive Positioning of Buildings

In some cases, buildings themselves were constructed with defensive features, such as elevated positions, thick walls, and narrow windows, making them easier to defend.

Hidden or Secret Passages

Some defensive buildings had hidden or secret passages within their walls or floors, providing escape routes or allowing defenders to launch surprise attacks on besiegers.

Hilltop and Cliffside Locations

Choosing hilltops or cliffside locations for fortifications provided a natural advantage, making it harder for attackers to approach and creating a commanding view of the surrounding area.

CAIRO'S HIDDEN GEMS

C airo, with its long and storied history, is a city filled with hidden gems waiting to be discovered by intrepid travelers. While the iconic landmarks like the Pyramids and the Egyptian Museum are must-visit attractions, there are many lesser-known spots and experiences that offer a glimpse into the city's rich cultural heritage. Here are some of Cairo's hidden gems:

Al-Muizz Street

Al-Muizz Street, also known as "Al-Muizz li-Din Allah Al-Fatimi Street," is one of the most historically significant and architecturally rich streets in Cairo, Egypt. Located in the heart of Islamic Cairo, Al-Muizz Street is a hidden gem that offers a fascinating journey through the city's Islamic heritage. Here are some key highlights of Al-Muizz Street:

Historical Significance

Al-Muizz Street dates back to the Fatimid period (969-1171 AD) and was the main artery of Cairo during that era. It was the royal procession route and served as a vibrant center for commerce, culture, and religion.

Architectural Marvels

The street is lined with beautifully preserved architectural masterpieces that span various historical periods, including the Fatimid, Ayyubid, Mamluk, and Ottoman periods. The buildings showcase stunning examples of Islamic architecture, with intricate facades, decorative motifs, and elaborate stonework.

Mosques and Madrassas

Al-Muizz Street is home to some of Cairo's most famous and historic mosques and madrassas (Islamic schools). One of the highlights is the Mosque-Madrassa of Sultan Hassan, an impressive Mamluk-era structure known for its grandeur and size.

Khan El Khalili Market

Al-Muizz Street leads to the iconic Khan El Khalili bazaar, a bustling marketplace that has been a center of trade and commerce since medieval times. Visitors can explore a variety of shops selling traditional goods, handicrafts, spices, textiles, and souvenirs.

Street Performances and Festivals

Al-Muizz Street is a vibrant and lively place, often featuring street performances, traditional music, and cultural festivals. It comes alive during special occasions and religious celebrations.

Religious and Cultural Diversity

The street is a symbol of Egypt's religious and cultural diversity, with numerous religious buildings representing different Islamic sects and historical periods. It reflects the peaceful coexistence of various communities in Cairo's past and present.

Preservation Efforts

In recent years, significant efforts have been made to restore and preserve the historical buildings along Al-Muizz Street. Restoration projects have revived the street's architectural glory, making it a UNESCO World Heritage Site.

Pedestrian-Friendly Zone

To promote tourism and enhance the visitor experience, certain sections of Al-Muizz Street have been designated as pedestrian-only zones, allowing tourists to explore the architectural wonders on foot.

Guided Tours

Guided tours and walking tours are available for visitors interested in learning about the history, architecture, and cultural significance of Al-Muizz Street. Local guides provide valuable insights into the street's hidden gems and historical context.

El Fishawy Café

El Fishawy Café, also known as El Fishawy Coffeehouse or Fishawy Café, is one of the oldest and most iconic cafés in Cairo, Egypt. Located in the heart of Khan El Khalili, one of the city's most famous marketplaces, the café has a rich history and is deeply woven into the cultural fabric of Cairo. Here are some key aspects of El Fishawy Café:

Historical Significance

El Fishawy Café was established in 1773, making it one of the oldest cafés in Cairo and possibly one of the oldest in the world. It has been a gathering place for locals, writers, artists, and intellectuals for centuries.

Traditional Atmosphere

The café exudes an old-world charm and retains its authentic ambiance, with vintage decor, antique furnishings, and traditional lanterns hanging from the ceilings. Stepping into El Fishawy feels like stepping back in time.

Architectural Heritage

The café is housed in a historic building that showcases traditional Egyptian architecture. Its arched doorways, intricately designed wooden screens, and traditional seating areas add to its unique charm.

Cultural Hub

El Fishawy Café has been a hub for artistic and intellectual discussions throughout its history. It has hosted numerous poets, writers, and thinkers, making it an essential part of Cairo's cultural landscape.

Shisha and Tea

The café is renowned for serving traditional Egyptian tea and offering a wide variety of flavored shisha (hookah), providing visitors with an authentic taste of Egyptian café culture.

Live Music and Performances

El Fishawy occasionally hosts live music performances, including traditional Egyptian music, creating a lively and enjoyable atmosphere for patrons.

All-Day Operation

The café is open 24 hours a day, seven days a week, making it a popular spot for locals and tourists to socialize, relax, and enjoy the unique ambiance at any time of the day or night.

International Fame

Over the years, El Fishawy Café has attracted a significant number of international visitors, including celebrities and dignitaries, further adding to its fame and allure.

Community Gathering

The café is a place where people from various walks of life come together to share conversations, laughter, and stories, fostering a sense of community and camaraderie.

Authentic Souvenir

For tourists, a visit to El Fishawy Café is not just about enjoying the atmosphere but also an opportunity to take home an authentic piece of Cairo's cultural heritage.

Bayt Al-Suhaymi

Bayt Al-Suhaymi, also known as the House of Suhaymi, is a beautifully preserved 17th-century Ottoman-era mansion located in the heart of Islamic Cairo, Egypt. It is one of the most significant historical houses in Cairo and offers visitors a glimpse into the traditional Egyptian architecture and lifestyle of the past. Here are some key aspects of Bayt Al-Suhaymi:

Historical Significance

Built during the Ottoman period in the 17th century, Bayt Al-Suhaymi served as a private residence for a wealthy merchant from the prominent Suhaymi family. The house reflects the architectural and cultural influences of the time.

Architecture and Design

Bayt Al-Suhaymi is a prime example of traditional Egyptian architecture, featuring a mix of Ottoman, Mamluk, and Islamic architectural styles. It has an elaborate facade, intricately designed wooden mashrabiya windows, and a central courtyard typical of traditional Arab houses.

Courtyard and Fountain

The central courtyard is a hallmark of traditional Egyptian houses. It features a marble fountain, surrounded by arcades and ornamental decorations, creating a serene and tranquil atmosphere.

Haremlik and Selamlik

Like many traditional Arab houses, Bayt Al-Suhaymi is divided into two sections: the haremlik (private quarters for women and family) and the selamlik (public quarters for men and guests). Each section is architecturally distinct, reflecting the gender separation and privacy norms of the time.

Decorative Details

The interior of Bayt Al-Suhaymi is adorned with intricate wooden carvings, colorful tiles, and decorative plasterwork, showcasing the craftsmanship and artistry of the era.

Heritage Museum

Bayt Al-Suhaymi has been converted into a heritage museum, displaying a collection of traditional furniture, textiles, artifacts, and historical objects that offer insight into the daily life and customs of the past.

Cultural Events

The house occasionally hosts cultural events, exhibitions, and traditional performances, further enriching the visitor experience.

Tourist Attraction

Bayt Al-Suhaymi is a popular tourist attraction in Cairo, offering tourists and locals alike an opportunity to step back in time and experience the splendor of Egypt's historical heritage.

Film and Television

Due to its well-preserved architecture and authentic ambiance, Bayt Al-Suhaymi has been featured in various films and television productions, further contributing to its cultural significance.

Darb al-Ahmar Art School

Darb al-Ahmar Art School, also known as "Al-Darb Al-Ahmar for Art and Heritage," is an art school located in the historic neighborhood of Darb al-Ahmar in Old Cairo, Egypt. The school is dedicated to preserving and promoting traditional Islamic arts and crafts, providing education and training for local artisans, and fostering an appreciation for Egypt's cultural heritage. Here are some key aspects of Darb al-Ahmar Art School:

Preservation of Traditional Arts

The school's primary mission is to preserve and revive traditional Islamic arts and crafts that have been passed down through generations. These arts include calligraphy, ceramics, metalwork, woodwork, weaving, and more.

Educational Programs

Darb al-Ahmar Art School offers various educational programs and workshops for both children and adults. Students learn the techniques and skills of traditional crafts from experienced artisans, ensuring the continuity of these ancient art forms.

Reviving Traditional Techniques

By teaching traditional techniques, the school aims to revitalize interest in these arts and ensure that the knowledge is not lost to modernization.

Empowering Local Artisans

The school plays a crucial role in empowering local artisans by providing them with opportunities for skill development, employment, and economic sustainability.

Cultural Exchange

Darb al-Ahmar Art School fosters cultural exchange and cooperation by hosting workshops and collaborations with international artists and institutions interested in Islamic arts and crafts.

Artistic Events and Exhibitions

The school organizes artistic events, exhibitions, and cultural festivals that showcase the work of its students and other local artisans, allowing them to display their creations to a wider audience.

Contribution to Community Development

The school's efforts in preserving traditional crafts contribute to the revitalization of the historic neighborhood of Darb al-Ahmar, promoting tourism and community development.

Promoting Heritage Tourism

By providing visitors with opportunities to witness the process of creating traditional crafts, the school contributes to heritage tourism and cultural appreciation.

Social Impact

Darb al-Ahmar Art School plays a role in social impact by engaging local communities and fostering a sense of pride in their cultural heritage.

Revitalizing Cultural Identity

The school's work in preserving and promoting traditional arts helps reinforce Egypt's cultural identity and showcases the country's rich artistic heritage to both locals and tourists.

Mosque-Madrassa of Sultan Hassan

The Mosque-Madrassa of Sultan Hassan, commonly known as Sultan Hassan Mosque, is a grand medieval Islamic monument located in the heart of historic Cairo, Egypt. It is one of the most impressive examples of Mamluk architecture and stands as a masterpiece of Islamic art and design. Here are some key aspects of the Mosque-Madrassa of Sultan Hassan:

Historical Significance

The mosque-madrassa was commissioned by Sultan Al-Nasir Hassan bin Al-Nasir Muhammad bin Qalawun, a prominent Mamluk sultan, in 1356 AD. It served both as a religious institution (mosque) and an educational center (madrassa) for Islamic teachings and scholarship.

Architectural Magnificence

Sultan Hassan Mosque is renowned for its imposing size, intricate design, and imposing façade. The building's grandeur and attention to detail reflect the architectural achievements of the Mamluk era.

Mamluk Architecture

The mosque exemplifies the Mamluk architectural style, characterized by soaring arches, massive domes, and decorative elements such as intricate stonework, marble inlays, and geometric patterns.

Massive Minarets

The mosque features two towering minarets that rise to a height of approximately 81 meters (265 feet). These minarets are among the tallest in Cairo and add to the mosque's imposing presence in the city skyline.

Prayer Hall

The interior of the mosque boasts a spacious and beautifully decorated prayer hall with rows of marble columns and an intricately designed mihrab (prayer niche).

Madrassa and Islamic Education

The attached madrassa provided education in various Islamic sciences, including theology, law, and grammar, attracting scholars and students from across the Islamic world.

Preservation Efforts

Over the centuries, the mosque has undergone various restoration and preservation efforts to maintain its structural integrity and historical significance.

Tourist Attraction

Sultan Hassan Mosque is a popular tourist attraction in Cairo, drawing visitors from around the world who come to marvel at its architectural splendor and historical importance.

Religious Significance

The mosque continues to be a functioning place of worship, attracting Muslims for daily prayers and Friday congregational prayers.

Nearby Attractions

The mosque is located in close proximity to other iconic landmarks, including the Citadel of Cairo, the Mosque of Al-Rifa'i, and the famous Khan El Khalili bazaar, making it part of a significant historical and cultural complex.

The Nilometer on Rhoda Island

The Nilometer on Rhoda Island, also known as Nilometer of Rhoda Island or Qibla al-Mida, is an ancient device used to measure the water level of the Nile River during the annual flood season. It is located on the southern tip of Rhoda Island, which lies in the middle of the Nile River in Cairo, Egypt. The Nilometer played a crucial role in ancient Egypt's agriculture, economy, and religious beliefs. Here are some key aspects of the Nilometer on Rhoda Island:

Historical Significance

The Nilometer dates back to ancient times, with the earliest structure believed to have been built during the reign of the Pharaohs of the Old Kingdom (around 2700 BCE). However, the current structure on Rhoda Island dates back to the Abbasid period (9th century CE) and was restored in the 10th and 14th centuries.

Function and Purpose

The Nilometer was used to measure the rise of the Nile River's water level during the annual flooding, which occurred between June and September. The Nile's flooding was essential for Egypt's agricultural prosperity as it brought fertile silt to the fields, ensuring bountiful harvests.

Measurement Scale

The Nilometer features a vertical column with graduated markings indicating the water level. The readings were recorded on a regular basis to monitor the river's height during the flood season.

Religious and Cultural Significance

The Nile River held great religious and cultural significance for ancient Egyptians. The flood's arrival was seen as a divine blessing from the gods, particularly the fertility god Hapy. The measurements were closely monitored as they influenced religious ceremonies and the distribution of land taxes.

Nile Inundation and the Famine Stela

In times of drought or unusually low floods, the Nilometer readings were inscribed on the Famine Stela, an ancient hieroglyphic text that detailed the occurrence of famine and prayers to the gods for intervention.

Access to the Nilometer

Today, visitors can view the Nilometer on Rhoda Island from a raised platform, but it is not open to the public for direct access.

Architectural Features

The Nilometer structure on Rhoda Island showcases typical Islamic architectural elements, with a square well and a domed roof.

Nile Monitoring Tradition

The tradition of using Nilometers to monitor the Nile River's water level continued for centuries, even after the decline of ancient Egyptian civilization. Similar devices were built at various locations along the Nile, each serving the same purpose.

El Darb El Ahmar: Crafts District

El Darb El Ahmar, also known as Darb al-Ahmar, is a historic district located in the heart of Islamic Cairo, Egypt. The area is renowned for its rich cultural heritage, traditional crafts, and historical significance. El Darb El Ahmar is a vibrant crafts district where artisans continue to practice traditional crafts that have been passed down through generations. Here are some key aspects of El Darb El Ahmar Crafts District:

Historical Background

El Darb El Ahmar is one of Cairo's oldest neighborhoods, with a history dating back to medieval times. It was established during the Fatimid period and expanded during subsequent Islamic dynasties.

Crafts Tradition

The district has been a hub for various traditional crafts for centuries. Artisans in El Darb El Ahmar specialize in crafting lanterns, woodwork, metalwork, textiles, pottery, and other handmade products.

Lantern-Making Industry

El Darb El Ahmar is particularly famous for its lantern-making industry. The district's lanterns, known as "fanous," are intricate and colorful, often made of colored glass and metal, and are a popular souvenir for tourists.

Local Artisans

The crafts district is home to numerous workshops and small artisanal businesses. Visitors can watch skilled craftsmen at work, creating beautiful pieces using traditional techniques.

Revival of Traditional Crafts

In recent years, there has been a revival of interest in traditional crafts, leading to increased efforts to support local artisans and preserve these ancient art forms.

El Muezz Street

El Darb El Ahmar is part of the larger Al-Muizz Street, a historic and culturally significant street in Islamic Cairo that is lined with beautifully preserved architectural gems, including mosques, madrassas, and other historic buildings.

Souvenir Shopping

The district is a treasure trove for souvenir shopping, offering unique and handcrafted items that reflect Egypt's artistic heritage.

Social and Economic Impact

The crafts district plays an essential role in the local economy, providing employment opportunities for artisans and contributing to the socio-cultural fabric of the neighborhood.

Heritage Tourism

El Darb El Ahmar attracts heritage tourists interested in experiencing traditional crafts and exploring the historic landmarks of Islamic Cairo.

Urban Development

Efforts have been made to preserve and revitalize the district's historical buildings, ensuring that its cultural heritage remains intact amid urban development.

Old Islamic Cairo Gates

Old Islamic Cairo, also known as Historic Cairo or Islamic Cairo, is a UNESCO World Heritage Site that encompasses a vast area of ancient and historically significant landmarks dating back to the Islamic era. Within this area, several gates and entrances serve as portals to the city's rich past. Here are some of the notable gates in Old Islamic Cairo:

Bab Zuweila (Zuweila Gate)

One of the most iconic gates of Old Islamic Cairo, Bab Zuweila was built in the 11th century during the Fatimid period. It served as one of the main gates leading to the city and is renowned for its impressive architecture, including two large minarets and a distinctive central arch.

Bab al-Futuh (Gate of Conquests)

This gate is located to the north of Bab Zuweila and was also built during the Fatimid period. It features unique decorative elements, including carved stucco and marble panels, displaying the artistic sophistication of its time.

Bab al-Nasr (Gate of Victory)

Positioned to the northeast of Bab Zuweila, Bab al-Nasr was constructed in the 10th century. Its design is simpler compared to the other gates, but it has historical significance as it was through this gate that Salah El-Din's forces entered Cairo during the Ayyubid period.

Bab al-Wazir (Gate of the Vizier)

Located to the south of Bab Zuweila, Bab al-Wazir dates back to the Ayyubid era. It stands as a smaller, less adorned gate but is no less important in historical context.

Bab al-Barqiyya (Barqiyya Gate)

This gate is situated to the northwest of Bab Zuweila and was constructed in the 11th century. It is considered one of the lesser-known gates in Old Islamic Cairo.

EGYPTIAN FOLKLORE AND MYTHOLOGY

Egyptian folklore and mythology are rich and diverse, drawing from the ancient civilization that thrived along the Nile River for thousands of years. These tales, beliefs, and traditions have been passed down through generations, shaping the cultural identity of the Egyptian people. Here are some key aspects of Egyptian folklore and mythology:

Ancient Gods and Goddesses

Ancient Egyptian mythology was filled with a diverse pantheon of gods and goddesses, each associated with specific attributes, powers, and roles. These deities played a central role in Egyptian religious beliefs and were revered by the ancient Egyptians for thousands of years. Here are some of the most prominent gods and goddesses in ancient Egyptian mythology:

Ra (Re)

Ra was the sun god and one of the most important deities in Egyptian mythology. He was believed to be the creator of the world and the ruler of the cosmos. Ra traveled across the sky during the day, representing the sun's life-giving power.

Osiris

Osiris was the god of the afterlife, resurrection, and fertility. He was also associated with the Nile River and the annual flooding that brought fertile soil to Egypt. Osiris was an important figure in Egyptian funerary beliefs and rituals.

Horus

Horus was the falcon-headed god of the sky, protection, and kingship. He was the son of Isis and Osiris and was often depicted as a falcon or a man with a falcon's head. Pharaohs were considered earthly manifestations of Horus during their reign.

Isis

Isis was a powerful goddess associated with motherhood, magic, healing, and protection. She was the wife of Osiris and the mother of Horus, making her a central figure in the Osiris myth.

Anubis

Anubis was the jackal-headed god of mummification and the afterlife. He was believed to guide souls to the afterlife and was associated with the process of embalming.

Bastet

Bastet was the lioness or cat goddess associated with protection, home, and fertility. She was also seen as a guardian of the pharaoh and a symbol of feminine power.

Thoth

Thoth was the ibis-headed god of wisdom, writing, and magic. He was considered the scribe of the gods and was associated with the moon and lunar cycles.

Hathor

Hathor was the cow-headed goddess of love, beauty, joy, and motherhood. She was also linked to music, dance, and fertility.

Ptah

Ptah was the creator god associated with craftsmen and artisans. He was believed to have crafted the universe through his thoughts and words.

Set (Seth)

Set was the god of chaos, storms, and disorder. He was often depicted as a mythical creature with the head of an animal that scholars believe could represent a mix of several different animals.

Creation Myth

The ancient Egyptian creation myth is a central narrative in Egyptian mythology that explains the origin of the world and the divine forces that shaped it. Like many creation myths, the Egyptian version presents a story of cosmic beginnings and the emergence of gods and the universe. While there are variations in different texts and periods, the core elements remain consistent. One of the most well-known versions of the Egyptian creation myth comes from the Heliopolitan tradition and centers around the god Atum. According to this myth:

The Primordial Waters

In the beginning, there was only the primordial ocean called "Nun," which represented the waters of chaos and non-existence. The universe was formless, and no land or living beings existed.

Atum's Self-Creation

Out of the chaos, the self-created god Atum emerged. Atum was often depicted as a human figure or as a serpent, symbolizing his connection to life and regeneration. He possessed the power of self-creation and was the source of all existence.

Atum's Act of Creation

Atum, through his divine will and power, initiated the process of creation. He brought himself into being by uttering his own name, symbolizing his self-awareness and creative energy.

Creation of Shu and Tefnut

As Atum spoke his name, he coughed and spat, giving birth to the deities Shu, the god of air and atmosphere, and Tefnut, the goddess of moisture and dew. Shu and Tefnut became the first pair of gods, embodying the elements necessary for life to flourish.

The Ennead

Shu and Tefnut, in turn, gave birth to the earth god Geb and the sky goddess Nut. These four deities, known as the Ennead, formed the core family of gods in the Egyptian pantheon.

Separation of Geb and Nut

Geb and Nut were originally united in a close embrace, representing the potential for life to arise. However, Shu, as the god of air, lifted Nut into the sky, creating a separation between heaven and earth. This created space for life to emerge on the land.

The Sun God Ra

Atum-Ra, the united form of Atum and the sun god Ra, assumed the role of the sun and traveled across the sky during the day, bringing light and life to the world.

Osiris Myth and the Afterlife

The Osiris myth is one of the most important and enduring narratives in ancient Egyptian mythology. It centers around the god Osiris, his death, resurrection, and subsequent reign as the ruler of the afterlife. The myth played a crucial role in Egyptian religious beliefs, particularly concerning the concept of death, resurrection, and the afterlife. Here are the key elements of the Osiris myth and its significance:

Osiris, the God of the Afterlife

Osiris was one of the principal gods in ancient Egyptian religion. He was associated with fertility, vegetation, and the Nile's annual flooding, which brought life-sustaining water and fertile soil to Egypt's farmlands.

The Betrayal and Murder

Osiris was married to his sister Isis, and his jealous brother, Set (Seth), coveted his throne. Set hatched a plot to kill Osiris and take his place as ruler. He tricked Osiris into lying inside a decorated chest, which he then sealed and cast into the Nile.

Isis' Search and Mourning

Isis, the devoted wife of Osiris, searched tirelessly for her husband's body. She eventually found the chest with Osiris inside, washed ashore in Byblos, Phoenicia. Upon her return to Egypt, she mourned Osiris deeply.

Resurrection by Isis

Isis used her magical powers and knowledge of healing to revive Osiris temporarily and conceive their son Horus.

Set's Betrayal and Dismemberment

Set discovered Osiris' body and, consumed by jealousy and rage, dismembered it into numerous pieces, scattering them across Egypt.

Isis' Quest for Restoration

Isis, along with her sister Nephthys and the god Anubis, embarked on a quest to find and reassemble Osiris' body.

Reassembling Osiris

Through their dedication and magic, Isis and her allies managed to find and reassemble most of Osiris' body, except for his phallus, which was lost in the Nile.

The Gift of Resurrection

The reassembled Osiris became the first mummy, and through the magical rites performed by Isis and Anubis, Osiris was granted resurrection in the afterlife.

Osiris as the Judge of the Dead

Osiris became the ruler of the underworld, known as the Duat. In this role, he presided over the judgment of the dead, weighing their hearts against the feather of truth during the "Weighing of the Heart" ceremony.

The Promise of Eternal Life

The Osiris myth gave hope to the ancient Egyptians, assuring them that a just and merciful afterlife awaited those who lived virtuous lives and upheld moral principles. The belief in resurrection and an eternal afterlife played a fundamental role in Egyptian funerary practices, including mummification and tomb construction.

Animal Symbolism

Animal symbolism played a significant role in ancient Egyptian culture, religion, and mythology. Many animals were considered sacred and were associated with specific gods and goddesses, as well as various aspects of life and the natural world. These animal representations were deeply ingrained in Egyptian beliefs and were depicted in art, amulets, and hieroglyphics. Here are some of the most prominent animal symbols in ancient Egypt and their meanings:

Scarab Beetle

The sacred scarab beetle, or dung beetle, symbolized the sun god Ra and the cycle of life, death, and rebirth. The scarab was associated with the rising sun and was believed to roll the sun across the sky each day.

Falcon

The falcon, especially the peregrine falcon, represented the sky god Horus. Falcons were symbols of protection, divine kingship, and keen vision.

Cat

Cats were associated with the goddess Bastet, the protector of the home, fertility, and women. They were considered sacred and were often kept as pets in households.

Cow

The cow was linked to the goddess Hathor, who represented love, beauty, and motherhood. The cow's nurturing and protective nature symbolized Hathor's role as a caring mother goddess.

Jackal

The jackal, specifically the black-backed jackal, was associated with the god Anubis, the protector of the dead and the god of mummification.

Crocodile

The crocodile was connected to the god Sobek, who symbolized the protective qualities of the Nile River and its annual flooding.

Ibis

The ibis bird was linked to the god Thoth, the god of wisdom, writing, and knowledge. Thoth was often depicted with the head of an ibis or as a baboon.

Lion

Lions were symbols of power, royalty, and protection. The lioness was associated with the goddess Sekhmet, a fierce warrior goddess and protector of the pharaoh.

Cobra

The cobra, specifically the Egyptian cobra or uraeus, represented the goddess Wadjet, the protector of kings and a symbol of royalty.

Vulture

Vultures were associated with the goddess Nekhbet, who represented the Upper Egypt region and symbolized protection and maternity.

Folktales and Legends

Folktales and legends are an integral part of Egyptian folklore, reflecting the cultural beliefs, values, and imaginations of the ancient Egyptian people. These oral narratives were passed down through generations and were used to entertain, educate, and explain various aspects of life and the world. While many of these tales have been lost over time, some have been recorded in ancient texts and inscriptions. Here are a few examples of Egyptian folktales and legends:

"The Tale of the Two Brothers"

This is one of the most famous folktales from ancient Egypt. It tells the story of two brothers, Anpu (Anubis) and Bata. The tale involves betrayal, transformation, and brotherly love. It also features elements of magical animals and divine intervention.

"The Shipwrecked Sailor"

This legend recounts the adventures of a sailor who becomes stranded on an island after a shipwreck. He encounters a mysterious giant serpent that eventually reveals itself to be a benevolent deity. The story emphasizes the importance of humility and gratitude.

"The Doomed Prince"

This legend tells the tragic tale of a prince whose fate is foretold to bring doom and destruction to Egypt. The prince's journey is filled with trials and challenges as he tries to escape his destiny.

"The Story of Sinuhe"

This is a literary masterpiece from ancient Egypt rather than a traditional folktale. It follows the adventures of Sinuhe, an Egyptian official who flees Egypt and finds himself in foreign lands. The story explores themes of exile, identity, and longing for home.

"The Contendings of Horus and Set"

This is a mythological tale that recounts the conflict between Horus, the rightful heir to the throne, and his uncle Set, who usurped the throne after murdering Osiris. The tale involves epic battles, divine trials, and the resolution of a divine dispute.

"The Prince and the Sphinx"

This legend involves a prince who encounters a mysterious and enigmatic sphinx. The prince must answer the sphinx's riddles to save his life and the lives of his fellow travelers.

"The Story of Wenamun"

This tale is a fictionalized account of the travels of a priest named Wenamun, who faces various challenges and adventures during his journey to retrieve timber for a sacred temple.

Jinn and Spirits

Jinn, also known as genies, and spirits are supernatural beings found in various mythologies and folklores, including those of ancient Egypt and the broader Islamic world. In the context of Egyptian folklore and Islamic beliefs, jinn and spirits hold significant roles and are often associated with tales of the supernatural. Here's an overview of jinn and spirits in Egyptian and Islamic traditions:

Jinn (Genies)

Jinn are sentient beings created from "smokeless fire" by Allah (God) according to Islamic belief. They possess free will, can be good or evil, and have the ability to shape-shift and become invisible. Jinn are similar to humans in that they can follow various religions, and some even convert to Islam. The term "jinn" is derived from an Arabic root meaning "hidden" or "concealed," reflecting their elusive nature. In Egyptian folklore, jinn are sometimes depicted as spirits inhabiting deserted places, ancient ruins, and tombs.

Spirits and Ghosts

In addition to jinn, Egyptian folklore and Islamic beliefs also include spirits and ghosts. These are souls or entities of deceased individuals believed to linger in the earthly realm. Spirits can be benevolent or malevolent, depending on the circumstances of their death and their relationship with the living.

Belief in Jinn and Spirits

Belief in jinn and spirits is widespread in various cultures across the Middle East, including Egypt, and is deeply rooted in Islamic traditions. While not all Muslims necessarily believe in the existence of jinn and spirits, these supernatural entities play a significant role in Islamic folklore, religious texts, and cultural practices.

Legends and Folktales

Jinn and spirits are common subjects in legends, folktales, and ghost stories. These stories often depict encounters with jinn or spirits, their interactions with humans, and their mysterious or mischievous behavior.

Protection and Rituals

Due to their potential malevolence, jinn and spirits are often feared in Egyptian and Islamic folklore. People may take measures to protect themselves from these entities through various rituals, amulets, and prayers.

Jinn in Islamic Texts

The Islamic holy book, the Quran, mentions jinn in several verses, describing them as beings created by Allah. One of the most well-known passages about jinn is in Surah Al-Jinn (Chapter 72), where jinn encounter the Prophet Muhammad and listen to his teachings.

The Marid, Ifrit, and Ghul

In Islamic folklore, jinn are often classified into different types. The "marid" are powerful jinn, while "ifrit" are considered a type of rebellious and malevolent jinn. The "ghul" is another type of malevolent jinn associated with desolate places and graveyards.

Festivals and Rituals

Egyptian culture is rich in festivals and rituals that have been celebrated for thousands of years. These festivals and rituals hold deep religious and cultural significance, and many of them have roots in ancient Egyptian beliefs and practices. Some of the notable festivals and rituals in Egyptian culture include:

Opet Festival

The Opet Festival was a grand procession in ancient Thebes (modern-day Luxor) celebrating the rejuvenation of the god Amun-Ra. The statues of Amun, his consort Mut, and their son Khonsu were paraded from the Karnak Temple to the Luxor Temple.

Wepet Renpet (New Year's Day)

Wepet Renpet marked the ancient Egyptian New Year and the beginning of the Nile's annual flooding, which brought fertility to the land. It was a time of celebration and thanksgiving for the blessings of the Nile.

Heb-Sed (Sed Festival)

The Heb-Sed was a jubilee celebration that marked the renewal of the pharaoh's power and rule after reigning for 30 years. The pharaoh participated in symbolic activities to demonstrate his continued strength and vitality.

Sham el-Nessim

Sham el-Nessim is an ancient Egyptian spring festival celebrated on the Monday following the Coptic Easter. It is a national holiday in modern Egypt and is a time for picnics, family gatherings, and enjoying the outdoors.

Ramadan

As a predominantly Muslim country, Egypt observes the Islamic holy month of Ramadan. During this month, Muslims fast from sunrise to sunset and engage in increased prayer and charitable activities.

Eid al-Fitr and Eid al-Adha

These are two major Islamic festivals celebrated by Muslims worldwide. Eid al-Fitr marks the end of Ramadan, while Eid al-Adha commemorates the willingness of Ibrahim (Abraham) to sacrifice his son Isma'il (Ishmael) as an act of obedience to God.

Coptic Christmas (Christmas Day)

Coptic Christians in Egypt celebrate Christmas on January 7th. The occasion is marked by religious services, feasts, and joyful gatherings.

Moulid al-Nabi (Prophet Muhammad's Birthday)

Muslims in Egypt observe Moulid al-Nabi to commemorate the birthday of the Islamic prophet Muhammad. Festivities include religious lectures, processions, and charitable activities.

Traditional Weddings

Egyptian weddings are elaborate and festive occasions, often lasting several days. They involve cultural traditions, music, dancing, and feasting.

Hajj and Umrah

Muslims in Egypt who can afford it may participate in the Hajj pilgrimage to Mecca and the lesser pilgrimage known as Umrah.

Folk Medicine and Folk Practices

Folk medicine and folk practices have a long history in Egyptian culture, dating back to ancient times. These traditional healing methods and practices were passed down through generations and were often based on local beliefs, superstitions, and natural remedies. While modern medical practices have become more prevalent in Egypt, some elements of folk medicine and folk practices continue to be used and valued by certain communities. Here are some examples of folk medicine and practices in Egypt:

Herbal Remedies

Herbal medicine is an integral part of Egyptian folk practices. Various plants and herbs are believed to have medicinal properties and are used to treat ailments such as colds, digestive issues, and skin conditions.

Amulets and Talismans

Egyptians have a strong belief in the protective power of amulets and talismans. These objects, often made from stones, metals, or other materials, are believed to ward off evil spirits, bring luck, or provide protection against specific diseases or misfortunes.

Cupping (Hijama)

Cupping therapy, known as "hijama" in Arabic, is an ancient practice believed to promote blood circulation and remove toxins from the body. It involves placing heated cups on the skin to create a vacuum effect and drawing blood to the surface.

Evil Eye Protection

The belief in the "evil eye" is widespread in Egyptian culture. To protect against the negative effects of the evil eye, people may wear blue beads or use other charms and amulets.

Henna

Henna is commonly used in Egypt for decorative purposes, especially during weddings and celebrations. It is believed to bring good luck and protect against evil spirits.

Cup of Coffee for Fortune Telling

In some rural communities, coffee grounds are used for fortune-telling. After drinking coffee, the dregs are left in the cup, and the patterns they form are interpreted to predict the drinker's future.

Garlic for Protection

Garlic is believed to have protective properties in Egyptian folklore. It is often hung at the entrance of homes or worn as an amulet to ward off evil spirits and illness.

Honey for Healing

Honey has long been used as a natural remedy for various ailments in Egyptian folk medicine. It is believed to have healing properties and is used for soothing sore throats and promoting overall health.

Salt for Purification

Salt is considered a purifying agent in Egyptian folk beliefs. It is used in rituals to cleanse and protect against negative energies.

Traditional Bathing Rituals

Some communities in Egypt practice traditional bathing rituals using special herbs and fragrances. These rituals are believed to cleanse both the body and the spirit.

Folk Music and Dance

Folk music and dance are vibrant expressions of Egyptian culture and traditions, reflecting the country's rich history and diverse regional influences. Egyptian folk music and dance have evolved over centuries and have been influenced by various civilizations, including ancient Egyptian, Arab, Nubian, and Bedouin cultures. These art forms continue to be cherished and celebrated in both rural communities and urban centers. Here are some popular examples of Egyptian folk music and dance:

Mawwals

Mawwals are a traditional form of folk vocal music, usually performed in a call-and-response style. They are often sung in gatherings and celebrations, accompanied by simple percussion instruments like the tabla (drum) and the arghul (double-pipe flute).

Zar

Zar is a traditional healing ritual with music and dance that is believed to cure spiritual ailments. It involves rhythmic drumming, clapping, and chanting. The Zar ritual is especially significant in Upper Egypt and Sudan.

Sufi Music

Sufi music is associated with the mystical Sufi tradition within Islam. It is characterized by repetitive chanting of sacred verses and is often accompanied by instruments like the oud (lute) and the rababa (string instrument).

Nubian Music

Nubian music is popular in southern Egypt, particularly in the region of Aswan and the villages along the Nile. Nubian songs celebrate local customs, love, and daily life and are often accompanied by traditional instruments like the simsimiyya (stringed lyre).

Bedouin Music

Bedouin music reflects the nomadic lifestyle of the Bedouin tribes in the deserts of Egypt. It often features storytelling through song and is accompanied by instruments like the rababa and the darbuka (hand drum).

Raqs Baladi (Belly Dance)

Raqs Baladi, commonly known as belly dance, is one of the most iconic and widely recognized Egyptian folk dances. It involves intricate hip movements, undulations, and graceful arm gestures.

Tanoura Dance

The Tanoura dance is performed by Sufi whirling dervishes. Dancers wear colorful, flowing skirts called tanouras, and the dance symbolizes a spiritual journey and union with the divine.

Saidi Dance

The Saidi dance originates from Upper Egypt and is often performed with a cane or stick. It is a lively and energetic dance, featuring foot-stomping and dynamic movements.

Nubian Dance

Nubian dances are vibrant and lively, often accompanied by rhythmic drumming and singing. The dance movements are symbolic of Nubian cultural traditions and social events.

Zaffa (Wedding Procession)

The Zaffa is a traditional wedding procession in Egypt, accompanied by music, singing, and dancing. It includes dancers, drummers, and musicians leading the bridal party to the wedding venue.

ISLAMIC ART AND CALLIGRAPHY

Islamic art and calligraphy have a prominent presence in Cairo, reflecting the city's rich Islamic heritage and cultural significance. As the capital of Egypt, Cairo has been a center of Islamic art and scholarship for centuries, and it is home to numerous historic mosques, madrasas, palaces, and museums that showcase the beauty of Islamic art and calligraphy. Here are some notable aspects of Islamic art and calligraphy in Cairo:

Cairo Mosques and Religious Buildings calligraphy

Cairo's mosques and religious buildings are adorned with exquisite calligraphy, showcasing the beauty of Arabic script and its importance in Islamic art. Calligraphy in Cairo's religious architecture serves both decorative and spiritual purposes, as it often features verses from the Quran, religious phrases, and praises to Allah and Prophet Muhammad. Here are some key aspects of calligraphy in Cairo's mosques and religious buildings:

Quranic Verses

Quranic verses are commonly inscribed on the walls, domes, and mihrabs (prayer niches) of Cairo's mosques. These verses are selected for their significance and spiritual importance to Islam.

Arabic Calligraphic Styles

Cairo's religious buildings exhibit various Arabic calligraphic styles, including Naskh, Thuluth, Kufic, Diwani, and others. Each script brings its unique aesthetic and expressive qualities to the inscriptions.

Ornate Illuminated Initials

Many mosques feature illuminated initials at the beginning of chapters or important sections of the text. These initials are elaborately decorated, showcasing the artistic skill of the calligrapher.

Decorative Borders and Frames

Calligraphy is often accompanied by intricate borders and frames, enhancing the visual impact and providing a sense of balance and harmony to the inscriptions.

Geometric Patterns

Calligraphy is sometimes integrated into geometric patterns and designs, adding complexity and elegance to the overall composition.

Spiritual Atmosphere

The presence of calligraphy in Cairo's mosques enhances the spiritual atmosphere of these sacred spaces, invoking a sense of reverence and devotion among worshippers.

Contemporary Calligraphy

In some modern mosques, contemporary calligraphic designs are incorporated, blending traditional Islamic calligraphy with contemporary artistic expressions.

Historic Madrasas calligraphy and decorative motifs

Historic madrasas in Cairo are known for their stunning calligraphy and intricate decorative motifs, which are prominent features of the architectural design. These elements not only serve aesthetic purposes but also hold deep religious and cultural significance, reflecting the rich Islamic heritage of the city. Here are some key aspects of calligraphy and decorative motifs in Cairo's historic madrasas:

Entrance Portals

The entrance portals of madrasas often feature elaborate calligraphy, welcoming students and visitors with verses from the Quran or invocations to Allah. These inscriptions are often beautifully carved in stone or stucco.

Inscriptions on Mihrabs

The mihrabs in madrasa prayer halls, which indicate the direction of Mecca, are adorned with calligraphy inscriptions of Quranic verses or religious phrases. These inscriptions often serve as a focal point of spiritual reverence within the madrasa.

Calligraphic Panels

Madrasa courtyards and prayer halls may display calligraphic panels, featuring verses from the Quran, Hadith, or other religious texts. These panels are rendered in various calligraphic styles, adding elegance and beauty to the architectural spaces.

Decorative Tiles

Ceramic tiles with intricate geometric patterns and floral motifs are commonly used in the decoration of madrasa walls, facades, and courtyards. These tiles serve as a form of decorative art and are often combined with calligraphic inscriptions.

Stucco Carvings

Stucco is extensively used in the ornamentation of madrasas, with calligraphic inscriptions and decorative motifs carved into the plaster. Stucco work may include arabesques, geometric patterns, and medallions, enhancing the visual appeal of the architectural elements.

Quranic Band Inscriptions

Some madrasas feature band inscriptions of Quranic verses that run along the walls or arches of the buildings. These inscriptions not only add beauty but also reinforce the religious and educational environment of the madrasa.

Mosaic Inlays

Some madrasas incorporate mosaic inlays with calligraphy and decorative motifs in marble or colored stones. These inlays can be found on walls, floors, and other architectural elements.

Minarets and Domes

Minarets and domes of madrasas are often embellished with calligraphic inscriptions and decorative patterns, creating visually striking landmarks in the city.

Pulpit (Minbar) Decoration

The pulpits used by the imams during Friday sermons in madrasa mosques are often decorated with calligraphy and intricate carvings.

Islamic Art Museums

Cairo is home to several Islamic art museums that house remarkable collections of artifacts, manuscripts, textiles, ceramics, and other masterpieces from different periods of Islamic history. These museums offer visitors an opportunity to explore the rich artistic and cultural heritage of the Islamic world. Here are some of the prominent Islamic art museums in Cairo:

Museum of Islamic Art

Located in the heart of Cairo, the Museum of Islamic Art is one of the most significant and renowned museums dedicated to Islamic art in the world. It houses an extensive collection of over 100,000 artifacts from various regions and historical periods of the Islamic world. The museum's collection includes illuminated manuscripts, metalwork, textiles, woodwork, ceramics, and glassware, showcasing the artistic brilliance and craftsmanship of Islamic artists.

Tareq Rajab Museum of Islamic Calligraphy

This private museum is dedicated to Islamic calligraphy and is located in the Heliopolis district of Cairo. It features a remarkable collection of calligraphic artworks, including Quranic verses, Hadith, and other religious texts, showcasing various calligraphic styles and scripts used in Islamic calligraphy.

Textile Museum

Though not exclusively dedicated to Islamic art, the Textile Museum in Cairo includes a noteworthy collection of Islamic textiles. Visitors can explore the artistry and sophistication of textile production in the Islamic world.

Islamic Ceramics Museum

This museum is dedicated to the art of Islamic ceramics and is located in the Gayer-Anderson House, a historic building near the Mosque of Ibn Tulun. The museum houses a stunning collection of Islamic ceramics from different periods and regions.

Beit El-Sennari

This cultural center and museum located near the Al-Azhar Mosque showcases Islamic art, culture, and history. It is housed in a beautifully restored Ottoman-era building.

Cairo's vibrant street art scene

Cairo's vibrant street art scene is a reflection of the city's dynamic and evolving cultural landscape. Over the years, street art has become an integral part of Cairo's urban fabric, with artists using public spaces to express their creativity, ideas, and social commentary. Here are some key aspects of Cairo's vibrant street art scene:

Social and Political Expression

Street art in Cairo often serves as a form of social and political expression. Artists use their works to comment on current events, societal issues, and political situations, providing a platform for public dialogue and reflection.

Murals and Graffiti

Cairo's streets are adorned with colorful and striking murals and graffiti. These artworks range from large-scale murals depicting historical figures to small, intricate graffiti with thought-provoking messages.

Revolution and Protest Art

Cairo's street art played a significant role during the Egyptian Revolution of 2011. Artworks created during that time expressed dissent, unity, and hope for change, making the city's walls a canvas for political activism.

Art, and calligraphy Galleries and Exhibition

Cairo, as a cultural hub, is home to numerous art galleries and exhibitions that showcase a wide range of artistic styles, including calligraphy. These galleries offer art enthusiasts a chance to explore the vibrant art scene of the city and appreciate the works of local and international artists. Here are some notable art and calligraphy galleries and exhibitions in Cairo:

Townhouse Gallery

Located in Downtown Cairo, Townhouse Gallery is a contemporary art space that hosts exhibitions, workshops, and cultural events. It showcases a diverse range of contemporary art forms, including paintings, sculptures, installations, and multimedia artworks.

Zamalek Art Gallery

Situated in the Zamalek district, this gallery focuses on promoting Egyptian and Middle Eastern art. It regularly hosts exhibitions featuring established and emerging artists, and it has a significant collection of calligraphic artworks.

El Bab Gallery

El Bab Gallery, situated in the heart of Cairo's historic district, showcases the work of contemporary Egyptian artists. It features various art forms, including calligraphy, and aims to support local artistic talent.

Mashrabia Gallery of Contemporary Art

Mashrabia Gallery is dedicated to contemporary art and often includes calligraphy-inspired works in its exhibitions. The gallery aims to bridge the gap between traditional and modern art in Egypt.

**5. Cairo Opera House

**The Cairo Opera House hosts art exhibitions and cultural events that feature a variety of art forms, including calligraphy. It is a renowned venue for promoting the arts and supporting artists in Cairo.

Art Talks Gallery

Art Talks Gallery is known for its focus on contemporary art and experimental works. It often features calligraphic artworks that push the boundaries of traditional calligraphy.

Mahmoud Mokhtar Cultural Center

This cultural center regularly hosts art exhibitions, including calligraphy shows, honoring the artistic legacy of the renowned Egyptian sculptor Mahmoud Mokhtar.

Egyptian Museum of Modern Art

While not exclusively dedicated to calligraphy, this museum in Cairo showcases modern and contemporary Egyptian art, and some of the exhibits may include calligraphic works.

Darb 1718 Contemporary Art and Culture Center

This center promotes contemporary art and often features innovative artworks that incorporate calligraphy and traditional Arabic script.

Biennale Cairo

Held every two years, the Cairo International Biennale is a significant art event that brings together artists from around the world, presenting an opportunity to experience diverse art forms, including calligraphy.

ITINERARIES

Here are three itineraries for exploring Cairo and its surrounding attractions. Depending on your interests and the duration of your stay, you can adjust these itineraries accordingly.

Classic Cairo Experience (3 Days)

Day 1: Arrival and Giza Pyramids

Morning: Arrive in Cairo and check into your hotel.

Afternoon: Visit the Giza Plateau to see the Great Pyramid of Giza, the Sphinx, and the Pyramid of Khafre. Explore the ancient wonders and take memorable photos.

Evening: Enjoy a traditional Egyptian dinner at a local restaurant.

Day 2: Cairo's Historical Gems

Morning: Visit the Egyptian Museum, home to an impressive collection of ancient artifacts, including treasures from King Tutankhamun's tomb.

Afternoon: Explore Old Cairo (Coptic Cairo), visiting the Hanging Church, the Church of St. Sergius and Bacchus, and the Ben Ezra Synagogue.

Evening: Experience a Sufi dance performance at a cultural center.

Day 3: Islamic Cairo and Nile Cruise

Morning: Explore the historic landmarks in Islamic Cairo, including the Citadel of Saladin, the Mosque of Muhammad Ali, and the Sultan Hassan Mosque.

Afternoon: Take a relaxing felucca boat ride on the Nile River and enjoy the beautiful views of Cairo's skyline from the water.

Evening: Shop for souvenirs at Khan El-Khalili, Cairo's bustling bazaar.

Cairo and Luxor Adventure (5 Days)

Day 1: Arrival in Cairo

Arrive in Cairo, transfer to your hotel, and rest.

Day 2: Giza Pyramids and Egyptian Museum

Visit the Giza Pyramids and the Egyptian Museum.

Evening flight to Luxor.

Check into a hotel in Luxor.

Day 3: West Bank of Luxor

Explore the Valley of the Kings, the Temple of Hatshepsut, and the Colossi of Memnon on the West Bank of Luxor.

Optional: Hot air balloon ride over Luxor at sunrise.

Day 4: East Bank of Luxor

Visit the Karnak Temple Complex and Luxor Temple on the East Bank of Luxor.

Evening flight back to Cairo.

Day 5: Departure

If time allows, visit any remaining sites or do some last-minute shopping.

Depart from Cairo.

Cairo and Alexandria Cultural Delights (4 Days)

Day 1: Arrival in Cairo

Arrive in Cairo, transfer to your hotel, and relax.

Day 2: Giza Pyramids and Egyptian Museum

Visit the Giza Pyramids and the Egyptian Museum.

Evening: Take an overnight train to Alexandria.

Day 3: Alexandria Sightseeing

Explore the Catacombs of Kom El Shoqafa, the Qaitbay Citadel, and the Bibliotheca Alexandrina.

Enjoy a stroll along the Corniche and visit the Montaza Palace and Gardens.

Day 4: Alexandria to Cairo

Visit the Roman Amphitheatre, the Alexandria National Museum, and the Mosque of Abu al-Abbas al-Mursi.

Return to Cairo in the evening.

MAPS

Metro Map

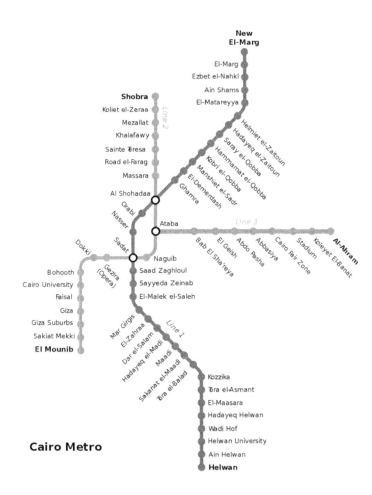

Cairo Metro

Street Map of Cairo

Nile River Map

Cairo Accomodation Map

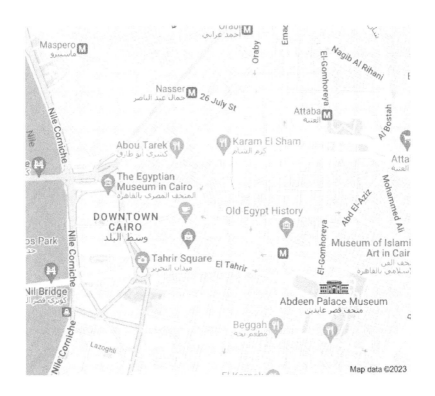

Restaurant and Cuisine Map

CONCLUSION

As we bid farewell to Cairo, we carry with us the memories of an extraordinary journey that transcends time and space. The city's magnetic allure, deeply rooted in its ancient heritage, will forever leave an indelible mark on our hearts and minds. Cairo's timeless wonders, from the enigmatic Pyramids of Giza to the vibrant streets brimming with life, have shown us the resilience and vibrancy of Egypt's cultural tapestry.

Through this travel guide, we have explored the splendor of ancient monuments, the beauty of Islamic and Coptic architecture, and the richness of Egyptian traditions and cuisine. We have witnessed the harmonious coexistence of history and modernity, as Cairo continues to evolve while preserving its heritage.

But our journey does not end here; it merely marks the beginning of an enduring connection to this captivating city. Cairo's allure, its mysteries, and its enchanting spirit will beckon us to return, to explore further, and to immerse ourselves in its ever-evolving story.

As the sun sets over the Nile, casting its golden glow upon the city's timeless silhouette, we carry with us the essence of Cairo—the essence of a place where history, culture, and life intertwine, creating a destination that remains eternally alluring.

Until we meet again, Cairo, with your enigmatic charm and warm embrace, we bid you farewell, knowing that your mysteries will forever beckon us to return and unravel more of your captivating secrets.

INDEX

Printed in Great Britain
by Amazon

26918779R00145